KEEP ON MOVING!

AN OLD FELLOW'S JOURNEY INTO THE WORLD OF ROLLATORS, MOBILE SCOOTERS, RECUMBENT TRIKES, ADULT TRIKES AND ELECTRIC BIKES

ALLEN B. BALLARD

CM Christopher Matthews Publishing

Keep on Moving!

Editors: Rob and Lisa Brill, Jeremy Soldevilla
Cover design: MJC Imageworks
Interior design: Lisa Madigan

PHOTO CREDITS

Title Page
    Alinker Image © The Alinker Inventions, Ltd.

Back Cover (left to right)
    Man on Alinker © The Alinker Inventions, Ltd.
    Rickshaw-Style Trike © Cycling Without Age
    Diverse folks Using Alinkers © The Alinker Inventions, Ltd.

Front Cover
    (top left) *Two Linked Trikes* © Hase Bikes
    (top right) *Downhill in Snow* © Ice Trikes, Inc.
    (middle inset image) *Author (Allen Ballard),* photo by © Ivan Steen
    (bottom left) *Woman on Alinker*, The Alinker Inventions, Ltd.
    (middle right) *Man in Blue,* © PFIFF, Inc.
    (bottom right) *Woman Enjoys Trike Ride,* © HP Velotechnik

ISBN 978-1-945146-49-7
ebook ISBN 978-1-945146-50-3

Published by

Christopher Matthews Publishing
www.christophermatthewspub.com

Printed in the United States of America

To friendship.

Acknowledgments

I would like to acknowledge and thank my brother, Walter Ballard and his wife, Marcia Ballard, Sheila Curran Barnard, Fred Bloom, Richard Hamm, Forest Hansen, Ron West, all of whom read the manuscript in its formative stages and made helpful suggestions. My fifteen-year-old "buddy," Michael Katongole, also made some suggestions and was of great help as a photographer's assistant. As always, Professor Leonard Slade was encouraging of my writing efforts.

I would especially like to thank Scott Pellett, CEO of Bike-On who not only gave me the opportunity to photograph bikes and trikes in his establishment but also went the extra mile to read the manuscript from the viewpoint of a seasoned industry professional. Of course, I alone am responsible for any errors that remain in the text.

I would also like to thank Dr. Anne Lusk of the Harvard T.H. Chan School of Public Health for her encouragement, and generous support.

I would also like to thank the following companies and persons for supplying me with photographs and permitting me to use them: The Alinker Inventions Ltd. (Samantha Jo Simmonds); Clarke Health Care Products(Susan Matuska); "Cycling Without Age" Inc. (Pernille Bussone); Day 6 Bicycles (Kelly Hutson President); Greenspeed (Ian Sims); Hase Bikes Inc. (Anja Wrede and Gina Wilbertz); HP Velotechnik Inc.(Heiko Truppel); Ice Trikes (Dan Pearce); Mission Cycles Inc. (Dean Wilsher); Motivo (Nicole Wolf); Pedego Electric Bikes (Nicole Schwartz); PFIFF Inc. (Kevin Wank); RANS Bikes, Inc (Kara Nichols);. Sun Bicycles Inc. (Anthony Avila); Superpedestrian Corp. (Jon O'Toole); Trident Trikes (Tom Flohr); Trionic U.S.A. Corp. (Oshin Mahmoodi); Van Raam (Inge Hummelink); and Bill Walzer, www.Bicyclebill, for his photo of the Bluebird. I was privileged to have Rob and Lisa Brill and Jeremy Soldevilla as my editors and thank them. I thank Reverend Charles Daniel and the Mount Calvary Baptist Church family for always being supportive, and Reverend Leonard D. Cominthier, Jr. and the Macedonia Baptist Church family for their video ministry to which I frequently now repair on Sunday mornings.

"It is hard to get old, have a parent who is getting old or serve those getting old, so read this book. Allen Ballard—who is 87, unable to drive, missing now-gone friends and mindful of one leg that has its own ideas—makes life better for all of us. He describes how to select the walker with Olympian assets, the adult trike that means freedom from the house and the route for the long morning and end-of-day rides. As only a retired professor can convey, he describes brakes, gears, crankshafts, seats and lights with more patience than the young bike-shop mechanic who has decided you clearly know nothing about bikes. Allen Ballard gives us a gift of happy years at the end."

—Anne Lusk, Ph.D., Research Scientist,
Harvard T.H. Chan School of Public Health

Table of Contents

FOREWORD

What's it like to face the aches and pains of old age? How should you cope with them? Throw in the towel, watch TV, take your meds and pray that the pain will go away? Or, instead, embrace your situation, keep a regular schedule, exercise and stay active in your community?

In this truly uplifting book, my good friend, Allen Ballard, explores the many avenues open to you to keep mobile, even as old age advances and seemingly narrows your options. There is indeed a wonderful world of mobility options waiting to be explored. Exercise and the great outdoors can turn your midnight into day. A rollator, for example, can extend your capacity to take long, invigorating daily walks. Adult tricycles and recumbent bikes can give you back the joy of childhood days in the sunshine. My friend explores these and many other possibilities as he fights, day by day, month by month, to keep his octogenarian body strong and vital.

Allen's clear and folksy writing style invites you to come along with him on this journey. No stiff and dry "how-to" manual is this, but rather it's an opening up of new vistas and mobility opportunities for seniors and others who might otherwise think they are destined to be housebound.

Living now as a retired physician of Ballard's age in a Sun Belt senior community, I try to play tennis at least three or four times a week, and I know the benefits —restful sleep, healthy appetite, weight management—that come from daily activity. I preach this gospel to my neighbors and friends. Yet, even I had not been aware of some of the personal mobility vehicles described in this ever-engaging and helpful book.

Unique in its information and analysis, *Keep on Moving!* is truly the first book I know of to explore the world of mobility devices from the standpoint of the consumer. I recommend it to you most highly, but with this one abiding caution: always check with your physician or healthcare specialists before engaging in new exercise activities or trying out any new mobility device. They must be the final arbiters of your pathway to health, but once they say okay, the sky's the limit!

George J. Amonitti
Hilton Head Island, South Carolina

INTRODUCTION

This is a book about my search to find alternative means of transportation and exercise when, two years ago, I was forced, at age 85, to stop driving. It was a bitter blow indeed. Cars were not only a means of transportation for me but a recreational hobby—I loved driving and followed automotive news avidly. But over the years, my body had worn down, so now I had to find some other means of going places. Neighbors helped out, and the new car services were available, but I wanted something I could call my own—a means of going up to the local cleaners, pharmacy and coffee shops. So I plunged into a search for alternatives to keep me mobile and active.

That search led directly to the writing of this book. I examined rollators, recumbent bikes, and electric bikes, all in an effort to substitute for the loss of my beloved car, my personal chariot. I knew that bicycles of all sorts are used for transportation and commuting in Europe. Why not here?

Before I knew it, I'd created a beginner's guide to alternatives to driving for the millions of folks worldwide faced with the problem of slowly declining health.

How can we keep moving? What choices are before us if we wish to stay active and in close communion with nature and the great outdoors?

In the course of the book, you, the reader, who may, in some cases, be a caring relative of the senior, will be introduced to various kinds of self-propelled mobility devices to help prolong an active lifestyle. Current as today's newspaper, it includes a chapter on the newest phenomenon—the e-bike or pedal-assist bike that bodes to become as popular in the United States as it is in Europe. In Belgium, for example, sales of e-bikes were close to 50 percent of the total in 2016.

What I've attempted to do here is to write a book that melds my personal experience with hands-on evaluation of various mobility devices. Blended in with the actual descriptions and alternatives available to the aging senior are my own experiences with various operations— hip, knee, and back—and the inevitable aches and pains that come with the passing of the years. There are anecdotes that will remind you of past physical trials and tribulations, but of triumphs too!

You may either choose to join me in this journey or, instead, opt to go directly to one of the evaluative chapters that might be of more immediate concern to you and your specific needs. I don't pretend to be an expert on all of these devices. For that the internet and consultations with your medical specialists await you, but I do hope this little book serves as a launching pad for your own explorations—it's full of hard-learned lessons!

Thanks for reading, and please stay in touch with me at allenballard@mac.com.

Disclaimer

This book's purpose is to provide general information to help individuals stay active as long as possible, but the author is not a medical professional, and the use of the personal mobility devices and bikes described herein can obviously result in possible injury, so the reader's choices and use of them should only be made in consultation with a physician or other qualified medical personnel. The reader, himself/herself, bears the ultimate responsibility for said choices and their usage.

Further, the writer and publisher disclaim any responsibility for any liability, loss, or risk incurred, directly or indirectly, as a result of information gleaned from this book. The author and publisher have made our best efforts to be accurate as to descriptions of the various devices and machines in the book but make no guarantees in this regard. Again, we cannot guarantee your satisfaction with the devices and machines described herein—it's up to you along with your medical team, to decide upon the appropriateness of their use for your particular level of health and conditioning, and the author and publisher can bear no responsibility for your choices in this matter.

Finally, the author is not an employee of any of the firms mentioned herein and has received no compensation, monetary or otherwise, from any of them.

Chapter 1
Are They Going to Take My License Away?

In my 85 years of life on earth, I'd never heard of a "certified automobile rehabilitation specialist," and didn't have the slightest idea what they did. But here I was on a late summer afternoon, in Schenectady, New York, about to face one. She would decide whether I ever drove an automobile again. Final exam time for a retired university professor, so to speak. The tables were turned now. My long romance with the car and the American road might soon be over. *Finis. Kaput!*

I thought back to the beginning, in Philadelphia, just after the war. I was in the driver's seat of my dad's Ford and the state examiner, clipboard and all, was in the passenger seat. We'd pulled up alongside a red Buick.

"Now back her in, son!" About 20 feet behind the Buick stood a parked blue Chevy. In between stood the impossibly small and cramped space into which I was supposed to maneuver my car.

An empty feeling came into the pit of my stomach, but I slowly backed up until my front bumper was about one third of the distance from the Buick's front, and slowly, oh so slowly, edged my way into the parking space, took my foot off the clutch, brought the car to rest, then engaged the parking brake.

"Good job," the examiner said. "Now for the big one."

With that, he pointed the way down to Philadelphia's City Hall and the infamous roundabout that still girds William Penn's building.

I came flying in from North Broad Street, into a veritable flood of vehicles, horns all honking at me, made it past the Parkway (Rocky's statue was decades away from standing at its far end), almost closed my eyes in fear, then finally emerged on the other side of the circle and headed back up Broad Street.

"Excellent, young man," he said. "Just get it home to the station, and you're good to go."

A half hour later, I emerged from the building with all the proper papers and my new license. My police sergeant dad was waiting, now seated in the driver's seat of the Ford.

"Congratulations. Let me see the license."

I handed it to him.

He looked at it, then put it in his wallet. "You passed their test, but not mine; you need another year of seasoning."

That was back in 1946 when I was a junior in high school, and a starting right tackle on the football team. I could run wind sprints up and down a field and still joke with the fellows when the session was over. Sometimes, if the coach caught me loafing, he'd put me right out front and make me lead the exercises. And I could do it with ease.

"Up, down, up down! Supnick, you're loafing!"

I went on to college, playing four years of football and lacrosse, enjoying the rough and tumble. I loved the days of spring with the sweet, new smell of

grass, bright sunshine and clear blue skies that hovered over the Ohio countryside. There also were the not-so-good days, with sleet and wind and soaked sweat socks, but there was always energizing camaraderie and the deep, satisfying sleep that follows extreme exertion.

I can't pinpoint when the actual impingement of my body's strength began, and don't really know when I began to get old. I did put on weight during my early 50s ballooning up to 250 pounds on a six-foot frame—too much drinking, eating, and stress. But I managed to turn all that around, and by my 60s was into a regular exercise routine.

I'd wake up at four in the morning in my Upper West Side Apartment, be in the pool at the mid-Manhattan Y by six, swim laps till seven, then take the bus over to my office on the East Side of town. Shortly afterwards, I began cycling to work on alternate days.

From time to time, I saw a strange sight: a tall, black man in a white sweatsuit jogging on the sidewalks of the Upper West Side. That was the first time I'd ever seen anyone jog anywhere. In the late '60s, nobody did that. He was a known fixture in the neighborhood, and I honestly believe he was one of the founders of jogging in the city, although I never knew his name.

One day, inspired by him, and trying to stop smoking (I'd even been to a hypnotist), I put on a sweatsuit in the Y, jogged up to Central Park and began to run around the reservoir. At first, I'd run for 15 minutes, then a half hour, and finally up to an hour. I was totally alone jogging in the park except for one woman. We'd exchange glances, and finally a hello, but that was all. I do truly believe that, along with our unsung hero whom, hopefully someday, someone will identify, we were among the pioneers of jogging in New York.

I stopped smoking, and jogging became the center of my life, my salvation from the real storm that was breaking around me with a divorce that consumed my very soul. My therapist nudged me along with these words: "It's impossible to be depressed when you exercise." So no matter the location—on the road for business or on vacation in the islands—I never changed from the routine of jogging

every day except to sometimes vary it with bicycling.

At times, in these early days of jogging, I'd receive very strange looks from the hotel staff when I came downstairs in my sweatsuit at six o'clock in the morning ready for my morning run. I'll never forget one stunning day, in Barbados on vacation. I jogged for an hour along glistening white beaches as the sun rose, seeming to emerge whole from the ocean as if God had told it: Time now to shed light on the world.

This became a lifetime pattern with me. Having moved to New Jersey in the '80s, I'd run a good five miles or cycle 10 miles every morning before taking the bus into Manhattan. I loved the early-morning hours and the good feeling of sitting down to a steaming bowl of oatmeal, flavored with cinnamon and butter. A hot cup of coffee and I was ready for the day.

When my knees first began to hurt, in my early 60s, I transitioned to walking, substituting a good half-hour walk for my standard three-mile jogging circuits, and I began to increase the time spent in the pool. By now, I was teaching at the University at

Albany. I became a habitué of its wonderful pool, putting in a good 45-minute session every day. But all of this exercise, although it kept me away from the cardiologist until this year (I'm 87 now), could not stave off the inevitable decline in my mobility.

I think it was around the time of 9/11 and the age of 70 that I had my first encounter with an orthopedic surgeon. After he'd done the first arthroscopic surgery on my knee, he prescribed a cane for the rest of my life. When I demurred, he said, "Use it and just fool the people and pretend that you're distinguished!"

That surgery was the first step on my way to modified mobility. About three years later, after long drives, I began to feel pain close to my groin on my right side and sometimes on my left side. It was a pain that steadily worsened until I could barely walk ten yards without wanting to sit down. I went to see the doctor again.

"You were a jogger, right?"

"Yes."

"The X-rays show it. Both of your hips are shot. Maybe we can save the left one. The right one may need replacement." He looked back at the X-rays. "But first, we'll try cortisone shots, they may help."

And "help," they did, administered every six months, for two years with the right hip and up to the present time with the left hip.

The time came for the right-hip replacement, and despite a "good recovery," my mobility was impacted. I really needed the cane at all times to maintain my balance, and though I could stride freely with it, walking became increasingly painful. I'd walk to the mailbox without the cane, a distance of about ten yards, and that was about my limit.

The cane slowly became a part of me. It was around this time that folks at the Y began to get on my nerves with comments like, "I didn't see you using the cane before. When did you start?"

I still kept up a lot of activities, including lecturing and serving as the head chef in my monthly stint in the soup kitchen at my church. I'd guess I was 75 years old then.

Five years later came the beginnings of numbness in my legs and again, a lack of mobility. This time, the diagnosis from another orthopedic surgeon was one of stenosis, a narrowing of the spine from old age. Walking, even with the cane, became even more difficult.

Again, the march toward surgery began with a series of cortisone injections in my back. Spaced out every four months, the shots helped. Then the day came, maybe two years later, when they didn't. It was back under the surgeon's knife for me, this time it was fusion surgery, which was successful in that it extended my mobility, still with the use of the cane, for another two years. I was pushing 80, and my leg movements were slower and slower, the feet more and more numb. Visions of a wheelchair appeared before me.

I was in my ninth decade, should have been retired, but I still enjoyed teaching, and the students—at least most of them—did not seem ready to run me out of the classroom that I loved so much. But I needed a way to get to class. Use of a cane over long distances was painful indeed. And it was a big campus, made for walking.

Enter the rollator.

Chapter 2
The Amazing Rollator—A True Walking Machine

As with all things, there's a history to the development of the rollator. Most of us are familiar with the old-fashioned walker that we see old folks using, particularly after surgery. It consists of a rectangular frame that one leans on and then lifts to advance step by slow step. Sometimes they have two wheels and two posts or—more often—just four solid posts that support your body. They are strongly built and stable, and very much needed in the first days after surgery because the first thing that the surgeon says is "Get moving." They want you out of bed and walking to avoid deadly blood clots. These utilitarian walkers were not to become popular until the '70s, although the first prototypes appeared around 1940.

Such walkers, while useful, are slow and hard on the shoulders if relied on for a prolonged time, and they are really not meant to replace the actual locomotion of a healthy adult. You can't stride with them because if you did, you just might end up tripping yourself as a result of their upright design—you don't walk inside them! But, indeed, after several of my surgeries, they were a practical adjunct to my recovery. I'd walk up and down the ward floors. Sometimes, even going five yards with them would seem a triumph for me. These walkers are highly portable, easily stowed in a car, and can move you from your vehicle to your office. They're just not an efficient way for moving over long distances.

The rollator, in distinction from the plain walker, has either three or four wheels, two handles, locking brakes, a seat which may double as a tray, and usually a basket or a pouch. It's a different beast from the standard walker. A U.S. government study indicated that in Denmark, almost 7 percent of the folks over age 56 used them, and in Sweden, about 4 percent of the total population had rollators.

The device, invented by a Swedish woman by the name of Aina Wifalk in 1978, was originally a brand name but has become a generic term. Wifalk, who, according to info posted by a Swedish museum, was born in 1928, was struck by polio in 1949.

This remarkable woman then worked among the disabled, constantly using her own infirmities and truncated nursing education, as a stimulus for creative thought about ways to make life easier for the crippled and lame. In the 1960s she developed a device for exercising the legs and arms of disabled wheelchair users. Needing a respite from her own pain and infirmities, she came up with the idea of mating a metal frame with three or four wheels as a means of support.

Generous of heart, she never patented the "rollator," but gave it as a free gift to the world. The device was developed by a joint governmental and business association and made its first formal appearance in 1981. Aina Wifalk received royalties from her invention, which she donated to charities. She was 55 when she died of cancer in 1983. Millions of people, young and old, owe their mobility to this remarkable woman whose name should be added to that of the world's medical pioneers.

What should you look for in choosing a rollator? Google the name, and you'll see dozens of offerings, with differences in price, country of origin and design features. Though your therapist or physician is best suited to advise you on your final selection, let me give you an overview of some features that, from my experience, seem important.

The first thing to look at is the size of the wheels. Smaller five- or six-inch wheels may be fine for indoor use but are hardly better than a standard walker if you are going to go any distance and particularly for using it as a real-life exercise machine. You see, I don't look at my rollator as a support, but as a true "walking machine," a device that elevates my walking to a level nearly equal to that of an able-bodied person. My students used to run after me with questions, asking me to please slow down.

Eight-inch wheels will better enable you to adapt to conditions you might find outdoors, such as grass or the dirt fields you'll encounter should you want to go see the grandkids' lacrosse game.

And check out the quality of the wheels—cheap plastic, high quality polyurethane or real rubber—it'll make a difference if you plan to walk any distance.

Next, check out the seat. Is it padded or not? And how high is it? The seat of an average chair is 17 inches. Some rollators come in different heights or are internally adjustable. With your back condition and beat-up knees, will you have the leverage needed to lift yourself out of the seat? When comfortably seated, your feet should touch the ground.

How wide is the chair? Is it comfortable enough to permit you to sit through a two-hour basketball game? Does it have a backstrap to give you support while watching an outdoor concert? Is the backstrap cushioned or just a piece of hard leather? Is the seat adaptable as a food tray? If so, are there convenient indentations for glasses or cups? If not, is there an accessory tray available? You might often find yourself moving food from your refrigerator to the countertop and

from there to your kitchen table. In effect, the rollator becomes a food caddy. Who needs a helper!

Must the seat always be in a horizontal position or does it collapse vertically to give you more space for your body and increase your ability to take long strides when walking?

What's the weight capacity of the rollator? Some, like the Dolomite Maxi, can support as much as 440 pounds.

Does it have a basket? Metal or cloth? Does the basket have to be removed in order to fold the rollator? And while we're on that subject, how easily does it fold. Do you have to twist knobs in order to do so? Or are there just a couple of levers, or nothing at all, making it easier for your arthritic stricken hands? Does it fold lengthwise in the center so that the resulting two halves of the rollator come together, making it a compact package and much easier to handle? This feature also makes it much more convenient to stow the rollator in social situations, such as in a restaurant or doctor's office. You don't want the rollator to take up any more space than necessary and surely don't want its bulky presence in a narrow aisle to cause some elderly person with a cane to stumble and fall. Time after time, restaurant personnel have thanked me when they've seen how quickly and neatly my Dolomite Jazz can be stowed away in a compact package.

How heavy is it? There's a big difference between a 15-pound and a 20-pound rollator for someone with back problems or a generally deteriorated body. Remember, you're going to have to lift this awkward piece of metal into the trunk of your car or park it in the back seat. In this respect, note whether the rollator has a locking lever or loop to keep it in a folded position when lifting it. Otherwise, it can break open on you just as you're placing it into the trunk.

Almost uniformly, cheaper rollators—though perfectly functional if they fit your budgetary needs—are heavier, have smaller wheels, grips of plastic rather than polyurethane or rubber and are difficult to fold. As to the grips, look at them carefully. Are they molded in such a way as to fit the contours of your hand or are they just plain bicycle-type grips? Your selection will make a difference when you are grasping it tightly, with great pressure,

as you'll do when taking your morning walk.

Finally, check the brakes. They should hold well on a small incline. If they're too weak, the rollator can run away with you on a downslope. And they should lock hard and firm when they are pushed downward so as to provide a stable foundation when you sit down on the rollator. That's called a parking-brake feature.

Incidentally, there are special "slow-down" brakes available as an option on some rollators, including mine. An adjunct to the regular brakes, they'll automatically slow the descent on an incline. In all cases, remember that rollator brakes, just like car brakes, can wear out. Mine did, and suddenly I found myself in trouble on a fairly steep incline and had to shove the rollator into a railing to brake it!

Rollators can be dangerous if not properly maintained. As with boats, it's the little things that can get you. Carelessly leave a line on a boat trailing in the water, and suddenly you'll find that it's tangled up with your outboard motor, and you have a seized engine. Walk along in a rollator with the brake cables not properly secured to its body, and you may suddenly find it torn from your grasp as the cables become entangled on a door knob or some other protrusion. Neglect to replace loose and worn-out rubber grips and you might find your machine slipping right out of your hands, and rolling away, out of your reach, down the hallway.

Be careful with your rollator at all times and remember that "slow and easy" is always better when moving from it to a chair or bed.

There are also some really specialized rollators, small indeed. You'll find them to be very portable but lacking some convenience features. My favorite in that category would be the Karman three-wheeler. This walker comes with a colorful pouch, weighs only 13 pounds, has very stable eight-inch wheels and collapses against itself into a very portable package. But it has no seat. This is not a trike that you would use for stride walking. You push it, rather than stand inside it. It's great for indoor use and in a confined space, such as a restaurant or place of worship.

I found my first rollator after a quick perusal of Craigslist. As is usual with me and to the everlasting detriment of my wallet, I had passed over the cheaper versions and settled on a Swedish model, made by one of the original companies—Dolomite. This rollator was practically brand-new, having been the last purchase of a recently deceased senior citizen whose declining poor health had made it impossible to use the device.

It was the Dolomite Maxi, made with a weight capacity of 440 pounds, a means for the most weight–challenged of all to keep mobile. It had a basket, was easily folded (though not in two halves) and was a dream to use as an exercise machine because its seat could be raised to a vertical position. You can literally step inside this walker, feeling as if it's an extension of your body when you move along at a rapid clip on your morning half-mile or mile walk.

It was a beautiful machine, with only one failing for my purposes. It weighed 21 pounds, which was a bit too heavy for me, with my various ailments, to easily toss into the trunk of my car. But I bought it for $50, which was a heck of price for a walker that routinely retails for over $300. It's still my go-to-machine for daily walks, sitting ready and willing right there on the front porch through good weather and bad.

Within a few days, I was exercising with my rollator, and making hour-long walks where, before, with my cane, I'd struggled to walk for 15 minutes. The rollator gives an instant sense of freedom, the same feeling that many of us old folks feel when we walk into a supermarket and first put our hands on a shopping cart. "Oh," the body says, "I've got something to lean on!" And almost immediately, we can stand erect.

I used the Maxi over the summer until suddenly I received an invitation to attend an important event at my alma mater, Kenyon College, that would require my making a trip using both an airplane and a rented car. Moreover, I'd have to do a lot of walking once I returned to my beautiful campus in the hills of Ohio.

For this trip, the Dolomite Maxi wouldn't do because I thought— though wrongly I believe now—that it would be a bit too heavy and awkward for easy airline travel.

Back to the internet I went in search of a more portable trike. I found "Wendy's Walkers," whose chief salesperson, a transplanted New Yorker, was down in Florida just waiting to assist me. He was a comforting old fellow who, it seemed, would rather have just chatted with me about the cold weather—"Is it snowing up there in Albany yet?"—than sold me a walker. But ultimately, that's what he did, after explaining the ins and outs of the various models he had in stock.

I can't overemphasize the need for a guide because, frankly, my local medical-supply stores either didn't have inventory to look at or were pushing one brand over another. They simply lacked floor space and seemed to know less about the rollators than I did.

And the stores seem to cater to the severely disabled, rather than to those of us whose joints are just gradually deteriorating. You walk into these stores on two feet, and they look at you in a weird way, like "Why do you need a walker, buddy?" How different from the obvious European enthusiastic embrace of rollators as a substitute for a cane and an exercise machine to extend folks' active life in the outdoors—a mobile ticket to better heart and body strength through daily exercise.

My newfound friend, Barry, steered me to the Dolomite Jazz. What a beauty it was! And, wow, at over $300, was it expensive! But worth every penny. With it, I can easily traverse the territory of Wal-Mart or Target in minutes, not a half hour.

put in place. So I'll digress a minute here. First, of all, the airlines treat you like a prince if you're disabled, and they are definitely geared up to make everything easy for you. But you must, at the time of booking your ticket, let them know about your physical condition. I did so and informed them that I would be traveling with my Jazz.

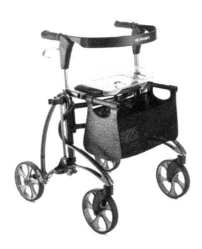

Fig. 2.1 Dolomite Jazz

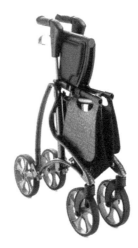

Fig. 2.2 The Jazz folds easily

This little gem, weighing in at 17 pounds, could be compressed into an 8½-inch by 20-inch package that could easily be loaded into a trunk of any car. And my maiden voyage with it was really an eye-opener for me and for my fellow airline passengers.

This was my first trip as a "disabled person," and I was a bit anxious about the various procedures the airlines had

When I was dropped off, now using the walker, I was met by a porter with a wheelchair. He packed me and the walker into it, checked my baggage, then left me free—at my request—to go through security with my walker. My tickets, cell phone and iPad all fit in the collapsible basket of my Jazz. I easily passed through security.

Fig. 2.3 *An afternoon stroll with a Jazz*

I stopped in at McDonalds for breakfast, walked down to the boarding gate and made myself at home. When the time came to board, I had priority status. I walked all the way to the cabin door with the rollator, where a flight attendant took it from me and stowed it away. As a mobility device, it did not count against my baggage-weight limit. Had I checked it with the rest of my luggage, its weight would have added to that total. So it's best to just walk right on down to the boarding station with your rollator.

Incidentally, my Dolomite was equipped with an optional cane holder and a nifty, little device called the "curb-climber," a small pedal next to the back wheel that, when depressed by your shoe, acts as a fulcrum to lift

the front wheels over a curb. This one amazes helpful bystanders all the time.

When we got off the plane, an attendant was waiting with my walker at the cabin door. He and several passengers looked on with awe as my walking machine expanded into a full-fledged rollator, complete with a folding basket, and a comfortable back strap. "That's some great engineering there!" said one.

Indeed, the Jazz was so comfortable that I was able to fall asleep in it while waiting to board the aircraft. Over time, I became a walking advertisement for Dolomite.

Surprisingly, one of my orthopedic surgeons inquired where he could order one for his dad. I was amazed at the question, but it indicates how some doctors, though skilled indeed in their professions are not aware of the startling advances that have been made in the development of mobility devices. To him, a walker was a walker. But old folks knew! They'd sneak a side peek at the Jazz, complete with its optional cane-holder, then shyly say, "Where'd you get that?" I'd smile and say, "You mean, where did I get this

BMW of mine?" We'd both laugh, then I'd launch into my praise of the Jazz.

Lots of alternatives to this modern marvel have appeared recently, but I've, of course, not yet had a chance to try them. And I'm surprised indeed that *Consumer Reports* has not yet seen fit to rank them. But Amazon is full of these new models, and they are the subject of numerous detailed reviews there.

One Chinese knockoff is the Drive Nitro rollator, which has many of the advantages of the Jazz but comes in at a price that is $100 cheaper. Both of these walkers share the distinction of being very stylish and give off a sense that you're active and strong. Indeed, if you're an old bachelor, they can actually serve as a means to start up a conversation and maybe get a date.

I increasingly used my Jazz as a walking machine. I could stand tall with it and feel like a natural man again. And there was absolutely no comparison between its utility and that of a cane. Indeed, I'm pretty sure that it was the continued use of the cane, the listing to one side, and the constant repetitive blows and jarring of the body that led to an almost unbearable pain in my neck.

I'd be sitting there, reading the paper, when suddenly there would come a jarring pain, akin to an electric shock. It would travel down my neck, lodge in my shoulder, then disappear into my left arm. It would come again at the slightest inclination of my neck. Pow! Like the devil was jabbing me with a pitchfork, and saying, "Ballard, the Good Lord has left you!"

Doctor's visits followed after treatments with ice and heat. They didn't help. The pain kept coming. Then came my exploration of a series of books by Robin McKenzie, who focused on proper posture as being a good preventive measure. Various neck exercises with an overhead strap and general strengthening gave some relief, but the pain, though diminished, continued.

I noticed that one particular machine in the therapy center, a bicycle-like arm exercise machine, really seemed to moderate the pain. I purchased a portable replica, a simple device that instead of pedaling, you rotated with your arms. I began using the machine three times a week for a half hour per session. The pain began to go away.

Then, one of my doctors prescribed a Derma patch. Now it might have been one or all of these interventions, but it was to my mind, the continuing reliance on the rollator rather than a cane that ultimately cured the pain because with the rollator, both shoulders are squared, and the pressure on the body is diffused.

We'll leave this introduction to the rollator with a parting nod to three other brands. The first is a startling newcomer on the rollator scene: the Motivo Tour. The second is the Trionic Veloped, and the third, the Alinker.

Fig 2.4 The Motivo Tour

The Tour, made in the United States, has to be called the Tesla of the rollator world. Aina Wifalk would be startled to see this truly visionary rollator—an original design that is almost a substitute car for the carless. It definitely borrows from the Dolomite's design and thus lets a user stand straight up, their legs inside of the machine. In addition, the makers of the Tour began with the thought that the rollator, although utilitarian, did not need to look—as some do— frumpy, like its users were on their last legs, so to speak.

It's unique and, befitting its style, a little pricey, listing at close to $500. Not only will you be able to do your daily walks with it, but you'll be able to do so with style and panache. There are spaces for a food tray, a cup holder and a built-in storage compartment for your wallet, smartphone, iPad and all the paraphernalia of the digital age. Like the Jazz, it folds into itself. And by dint of a covered frame, it both gives you a sense of privacy and a solid surface on which to display graphics that can personalize your walker with logos of your favorite teams, photos of beautiful lakes or any classy design. The options are endless, limited only by the imagination of its owner.

The front cover morphs into a full back for the seat. Unlike some other walkers, there's no need for a back strap because you have a solid, comfortable, tub-like chair to sit in. But it is, at around 20 pounds, a bit heavy.

Fig. 2.5 The Trionic Veloped Tour

The very expensive **Trionic Veloped** is a different creature altogether. Sometimes advertised as an alternative to the rollator, it's a Swedish-designed, Chinese-manufactured triangular-shaped vehicle with two rear wheels and a front bi-wheel, all oversized. It's particularly suited for use on grass and dirt, where a regular four-wheel rollator might struggle to adapt to the demands of uneven terrain.

With assembled weights ranging from around 27 to a high of 33 pounds, these are not easily tossed into the back seat of a car. Trionic has neatly solved this problem by a quick-release feature for the wheels. Without the wheels and heavy tires (they're pneumatic), the relative weights of the Veloped diminishes to 17-18 pounds, competitive with regular rollators.

It must be said that the Velopeds, running over the $1,000 mark in price, are heavily featured, well-made and particularly suited to outdoor use. For example, though the Jazz needs a curb-climber, the Veloped's much larger and specially developed wheels and tires—12-14 inches—will easily roll up over a typical curb.

Fig. 2.6 Veloped climbs a curb

Not to be outdone by the competition, Trionic has recently put out a series of rollators distinguished by oversized tires—9, 12, 14 inches—and synchronized front wheels to avoid the "squiggle" that can sometimes take place when pushing a rollator rapidly on an uneven surface, say, a cobblestone street.

Fig. 2.7 Trionic Walker

They're a few pounds lighter than the Veloped, slightly less expensive, and like it, have easily removable wheels. With a standard 10-year guarantee, Trionic designates its machines as premium. They're definitely in a class by themselves, but to persuade yourself to buy one, you'll have to repeat to yourself—several times—Benjamin Franklin's advice that,

"the bitterness of poor quality remains long after the sweetness of low price is forgotten." Who knew that driving a rollator could be so much fun and cost so much!

Fig. 2.8 Trionic Walker 9er Folded

Well, someone indeed knew, and her name was Barbara Alink, a Dutch woman whose company has developed a revolutionary rollator-like device called, appropriately enough, **the Alinker**.

Fig. 2.9 Moving along on an Alinker.

This self-propelled mobility machine is a "walking trike." In effect, the rider mounts upon a trike with two large front wheels, a small back wheel, a set of handlebars and a bicycle saddle, and then proceeds to push forward using feet instead of pedals.

Fig. 2.10 Alinkers

It's ingenious, for, at one fell swoop, the rider finds it possible to take giant steps where, previously, they could barely take one. Try to remember those times when you were a kid, took your feet off the bike pedals, pushed off with your legs and glided along for a few yards before doing it again. After watching some videos of this machine, it's pretty obvious that it will definitely—all things being equal—move at a speed two to three times that of a rollator. And the machine relieves the pressure sometimes

exerted on your shoulders and hands by a rollator. Upright on the Alinker, you push and stride, push and stride, literally moving into a true exercise rhythm. I can easily see this device someday being used as the basis for a Paralympic event.

The Alinker is heavy, weighing in at 26 pounds. That's a load for lots of senior citizens, but the trike folds and the wheels and saddle are easily removed for stowing in the back of a car. Its weight in this state is only 19 pounds, still not light, but only a couple of pounds more than my Jazz. Its weight capacity is 275 pounds and its price—sit down now—is a whopping $1,995. It comes with a two-year warranty and, if you go to the manufacturer's site, some financing alternatives.

Fig 2.11 Van Raam 'City Walker'

It's definitely worth it, says John Dawson of New Zealand in a government publication. A sufferer from MS for 40 years, he said that the Alinker bike changed his life, giving him the ability to move freely and making him feel "more fit and strong," so much so that now, for the first time in 15 years, he was able to go walking with his wife and "to have the opportunity to be outside again."

Chapter 3
The Ins and Outs of Mobility Scooters

A year before purchasing the walker, the folks at my job had stationed me at a distant classroom, maybe a good half mile from my office. I knew I couldn't make that distance back and forth, three times a week, with the use of the cane alone. My mind was still good, at age 80, and I could even pace back and forth in front of the classroom, puncturing the air with my cane, but a half mile was a bit of a stretch.

I was all set to retire, when suddenly one day, I saw a librarian friend of mine go sailing by on a little red scooter. She was sitting low and reclined in the seat, and I really felt sorry for her. She stopped, and always one to be helpful, said, "I broke my leg, and the university lent me this one to use until it heals. You ought to try one. You could definitely use it."

I said, "Naw, I don't need that, but thanks anyhow."

Being an alpha male, I just didn't want to be looked down upon by everybody, because that's what it feels like when you're sitting low in a mobile scooter like you're an automatic target of pity. But as the summer rolled on, and the prospect of walking that long distance loomed large, I had second thoughts about using a mobility scooter.

After extensive internet research about them, I went to Craigslist, found a **Golden Technology Scooter** that cost $2,400 retail, and was able to purchase it for $850 brand-new.

As was to be the case with the walker, the fellow who sold it to me had purchased it for his dad who, with a failing heart, had never been able to use it. That seems to be the sad case with so many of the disability devices appearing on Craigslist and auction sites.

Deciding on one of these scooters is much easier than choosing a walker. After all, these machines are so simple to operate that they are found in most big-box stores. Most of them will be foolproof because usually, the only maintenance necessary is to keep the battery charged and have the machine lubricated yearly.

One has to consider too whether it should be a four-wheel or three-wheel scooter. The former will be more unwieldy and better suited for outdoor use, the latter good for inside buildings and homes.

I think the only major issue concerning motor scooters is their relative portability or lack thereof. A larger, more robust scooter such as my Golden cannot be easily transported, save with a specially equipped vehicle. There are, however, portable scooters that break down for easy stowing in the trunk of a car. Usually, such a scooter will have a smaller battery and thus, a shorter range than the non-portable models. Even when broken down, the pieces of the scooter may be too heavy for a handicapped person to handle alone—even the light ones are heavy machines. For example, the Lexis Light, which advertises itself as the "world's lightest scooter," at 54 pounds, breaks

down into two sections: one of 26 pounds, the other 28 pounds.

You should check too on the ability of the scooter to navigate doorways within your house. In all cases, the scooter should have a light, a horn and some kind of a basket. It should, ideally, have a seat that not only reclines but also swivels right and left for easy mounting and accessibility. It goes without saying that the seat should be comfortable and cushiony, something that would evoke a sense of pleasure when you sink into it.

Check too on the method of charging the battery. Some batteries on the more portable models are removable and can easily be charged without moving the scooter. Others cause you to reach down low because the heavy battery is encased in the body of the scooter and its cord has to be plugged into a floor-level outlet. This can be hard on one's back. More modern models have a high charging point built into the scooter itself, making it a lot easier to make the connection. Finally, check too to see if the scooter has provisions for a cane or crutches holder. Indeed, I've seen some scooters with a walker holder, serving up a one-two mobility punch. All the comforts of home.

You should also consider the range of the scooter. Mine on a fully charged battery goes up to 15 miles, and I routinely would use it around campus for two weeks or so without recharging.

I grew to love my mobility scooter, particularly on days when I was a bit tired from teaching several classes. It moved me quickly from one classroom to another, and after a while, I became as attached to it as folks two centuries ago might have become attached to their horses. I'd just turn the key in that scooter and off I went to class or seminar or evening concert on campus. And sometimes, when I became a bit tired, I'd just sit down in it and continue my lecture. It was very comfortable and thank goodness I never fell asleep in it while pontificating!

Folks used to love to wave at me as I tooled around the place. The students rushed to open doors for me when I was unable to use my cane to push the automatic door openers. And I definitely overcame any semblance of guilt or shame associated with my disability. I was getting old, and I needed a good means of transportation.

However, in my last years of teaching, I came to rely more upon my Dolomite walker than my scooter for the former had the advantage of forcing me to do my daily exercise, and that was a great benefit indeed. Upon retirement, I turned the scooter over to the university for its use. I wanted to emphasize to myself the need to remain mobile through the use of the rollator.

Chapter 4
Fateful Encounter with an Auto Examiner

After my hip operation in 2007 at age 77, and my back operation in 2012 at 82, it took maybe six weeks before I felt able to drive again. On both occasions, I felt no compunction about getting behind the wheel again. When fully recovered, I'd routinely do road trips of 600 miles with no physical aftereffects whatsoever.

But slowly, over that time period, despite continued cortisone shots (yes, they were necessary for my back even after surgery) the right lower side of my body became numb. The right leg gave me the most trouble—always with an undifferentiated pain that stretched from the upper part of my hip down to the foot. The trip to the mailbox became more difficult.

Then came May 29, 2016. It was a Sunday afternoon after church. I'd just pulled up at a Dunkin' Donuts drive-through behind a Toyota Rav4. I

stopped the car. The Rav4 inched forward a foot or so. I went to take my foot off the brake to hit the accelerator when suddenly my Infiniti SUV eased forward. Somehow or another, my neuropathy-impacted foot had leapt off the brake and struck the accelerator before I'd intended to do so. Fortunately, instinct kicked in. I hit the brake, and the car halted.

My 13-year-old mentee in the back seat blurted out: "Oh, you did it again!" Michael was an honor student and a budding lacrosse defenseman. About three months earlier, after a stop at a convenience store, I'd just put the car in reverse, when suddenly it accelerated at about 30 miles an hour. I frantically jabbed at the floor. Somehow or other, my foot hit the brake, and the car screeched to a halt.

Only the good God Almighty had spared me from killing someone. Not 40 feet behind me and slightly to the left rear of the Infiniti was a man. He stood shaking his fist at me. I waited until he had safely passed the rear of the car, then stuck my head out of the window.

"Sorry, mister."

He must have recognized my age. "Damn it, fellow, you need to quit driving."

I must have been about seven years old when I witnessed my first vehicle accident. It was two o'clock on a Saturday afternoon. My great-aunt was holding me tightly by the hand as we walked through the small shopping center district of the Philadelphia neighborhood of Germantown. The stores were full of Easter shoppers. My aunt and I had just come out of a shoe store that had a most magnificent machine—a fluoroscope that showed you the outlines of your feet. The salesman had actually lifted me up by my shoulders, placed me on the contraption and, when he observed the size of my feet, said, "Wow, you're really going to be a big fellow, young man."

My grand-aunt—childless—had beamed down on me. "Yes," she said, "he's going to grow up to be a fine young man."

The motorcycle came roaring down the street so fast that I could only see a blur out of the corner of my eye. Then I heard a thump and a scream and saw a teenage girl's body being tossed through the air like a ragdoll. She landed not five feet from me. I can still see her eyes, startled, frightened, and looking straight at me.

My aunt's arms enfolded me, and she pulled my head up against her body. "Junie, don't look, don't look!" That evening, I overheard her telling my uncle about the girl who'd been hit and died right by the Rialto movie theater.

After the Dunkin' Donuts incident, I drove straight home and grounded myself. I thus became one of thousands of senior citizens who either voluntarily quit or are forced to stop driving.

You don't have to search far to find an example of an elderly driver killing someone. In 2014, in Brandenton, Florida, a 79-year-old woman mistook the accelerator for the brake, killed three fellow parishioners and seriously injured four others. In 2017, in Washington County, Florida, an 80–year-old woman died when her car spun off the highway and banged into two trees.

In 2015, according to Caring.com, an organization focusing on the needs of older adults, an astounding 14 million people under age 64 were involved in a car crash caused by a person aged 65 or over. An earlier survey by them indicated that almost 40 percent of folks under the age of sixty-five said they'd rather talk about "funeral arrangements than to talk with parents about taking away the car keys."

So who should decide when it's time to stop driving? Among respondents to a random nationwide phone survey by Caring.Com in 2015, 29 percent said they think a doctor is the best person to determine when it's time, while 25 percent said it should be a family decision, and 23 percent thought the government or local department of motor vehicles should decide. Only 16 percent thought the seniors should decide for themselves. Yet, a 2002 report in the *American Journal of Public Health* concluded, "In general, older drivers decide for themselves when to quit, a decision that often stems from the onset and progression of medical conditions that affect visual, physical and cognitive functioning and consequently driving skill."

Are senior drivers at risk on the road? Well, an AAA statistical study of 2012 tell us that crash figures are highest for 16-17-year-olds, then diminish steadily before leveling off at age 65. They begin to rise slightly at ages 70-75 before becoming a definite factor for those over 85. The latter group has the highest rate of auto fatalities. Seniors, by and large, adapt to their increasing infirmities by cutting down on automobile use and carefully choosing their time and place of driving. Nevertheless, according to the Centers for Disease Control, "In 2015, more than 6,800 older adults were killed and more than 260,000 were treated in emergency departments for motor vehicle crash injuries. This amounts to 19 older adults killed and 712 injured in crashes on average every day."

What's the cause? Quite simply, old age and its accompanying physical and mental disabilities although all seniors don't age at the same rate, and each one surely deserves to be evaluated without reference to their calendar years. According to a 2015 medical professional guide available on GeriatricsCare.com, some 60 percent of drivers over 85 had cars as their sole means of transportation. One can envision immediately the social, psychological and economic impact that ensues from car deprivation. Nevertheless, according to a 2017 study in *Rheumatology International*, half of Americans over 65 have some form of arthritis and a good 18 percent of individuals aged 75-84 had Alzheimer's disease dementia, while 22 percent of folks over 71 had some milder form of cognitive impairment.

It's not surprising then that a 2015 insurance study by the IIHS found: "71 percent of older drivers' inadequate surveillance errors were due to looking and not seeing another vehicle or failing to see a traffic control rather than failing to look, compared with 40 percent of inadequate-surveillance errors among middle-aged drivers. "It concluded, "Errors older drivers commonly make stem from the typical issues associated with aging. These include declines in cognitive, perceptual and physical abilities."

AARP notes the following signs that the senior should consider turning in their license:

- Delayed response to unexpected situations
- Becoming easily distracted while driving
- Decrease in confidence while driving
- Having difficulty moving into or maintaining the correct lane of traffic
- Hitting curbs when making right turns or backing up
- Getting scrapes or dents on car, garage or mailbox
- Having frequent close calls
- Driving too fast or too slow for road conditions

But some folks never want to give up. I was down in Florida a few years back, outside of a food market in a big mall, when suddenly I saw a beautiful Mercedes 450SL convertible come driving down the street. It didn't seem to have a driver, but suddenly I saw a man behind the wheel. His golf cap appeared to be resting on the wheel. The man was not able to keep his neck up straight. He drove past me, took a turn and before I knew it, he was back again. The guy was cruising around the parking lot looking for pick-ups and couldn't keep his head up.

I had effectively grounded myself from driving but definitely had not given up. It's a strange feeling to wake up one morning and know that one of the loves of your life, cars, had been taken away from you.

Fortunately, for me, there was no immediate economic impact because I had just taught my last lecture in a very long academic career. But other questions immediately came to mind. How was I to make it to church on Sunday? How was I going to get to the library and the books that had been so central to my life? What about the doctors, the internist, the orthopedic surgeon, the podiatrist, the ear doctor, the dentist? They were all located a good 15 miles from my home in Clifton Park. How was young Michael going to get to his sports events? What about the food shopping, McDonalds, coffee from Dunkin' Donuts and the small summer camp up at Lake George, 100 miles away?

There had to be a better way. I knew that huge advances had been made with the creation of hand controls for the disabled, so I

immediately set to work researching them. It seemed a good solution to my transportation problem. My doctor even suggested their use to me.

The simplest of these machines consist of levers attached to the steering post, then connected to one end of a long rod. On the other end, metal clamps are affixed to the brake and accelerator of the car. This is a simple mechanical device, almost foolproof in its execution. Generally, they are operated by varying motions of the hand, say a forward motion for the brake and a downward one for the accelerator. One of the most popular of these machines is the **MPS Monarch**.

There are naturally many variations on these mechanisms, and their prices change accordingly. You may find one at $700 or another far more expensive, full of software that bypasses the accelerator and is wired directly into the engine of the car. And some specially fitted cars totally eliminate a steering wheel and substitute a joystick, much as you find in a video game.

The automotive industry has placed great emphasis on finding solutions for drivers with disabilities. A quick look at

YouTube and Amazon showed an amazing variety of these instruments, many capable of being home-installed if suitable assistance were available for the impaired person.

Encouraged by my survey, I made a call to a local shop that specialized in hand controls and had a good conversation with a technician who actually gave me a decent installed price of around $1,500 for a basic system. But then he threw a wrench into the works. "Unfortunately," said he, "you've got to be recommended by an automobile occupational therapist, and only then can I help you. That's the rules."

A perusal of the New York State Department of Motor Vehicles site made it clear that I was in a mess of trouble. The occupational therapist's job was to evaluate my medications, knowledge of rules, physical and mental condition, and decide if I was fit to drive a car. In short, I had to run a gauntlet when I already knew that my bum right leg was the problem.

The whole process was not easy. First, I had to obtain a prescription from my doctor to have the local rehab center, in my case, Sunnyview in Schenectady, do the evaluation. Second, there was a three-month waiting list. Third, the evaluation cost $400 and was not covered by my health insurance.

On the day of the evaluation, I was as nervous as a youngster going to his first day in school. While I was waiting for the therapist, a tall, gangly man of about 80, obviously impaired by a stroke, was led in by his much younger wife. She guided him with a curt order: "Don't sit down too quickly. I don't want you to fall again. Remember the last time."

After he was seated, blithely ignoring his presence, she said to me: "He was a strong man, farmed all his life, and I think he hates everything now." Upon learning that I was to take the driver's test, the lady gave me the great news that her husband had taken the same test about three years earlier and flunked it. "It was one hell of a struggle to get him to come here, so strong-willed." All the while, seemingly oblivious of her comments, the poor fellow looked straight ahead.

Finally, the occupational therapist arrived, head bent over the medical records sent over my doctor. She was very capable and very direct. "This way, please. We're going to see if we can keep you on the road."

After an examination of my general physical condition, eye tests and a written exam on rules of the road, the therapist seated me on a driving simulator. Dangerous scene after dangerous scene appeared before me: a toddler chasing a ball into the street; a horse-drawn farm wagon filled with hay slowing down traffic; a truck ignoring a stop sign. Sirens blared, and ambulances careened down the road. After the last event—barriers lowering over a railroad track—the test was over.

She studied her screen, then smiled. "You're doing great so far. Your reflexes are fine." She made some notations on her computer.

I was beginning to warm up to this examiner, even had her talking about the uniqueness of her profession and some of the truly serious problems that were brought to her. But then, pulling out a little hammer, she asked me to place my feet on a stool. She tapped on the sole of my shoe with the motion of a doctor checking your reflexes.

"Tell me when you feel it."

She must have struck about 10 blows before I finally said, "I felt that one."

"Good. About 95 percent of the people in this country would have reacted before then." She shook her head. "You're finished driving any car with an accelerator, but there's still the possibility of the hand controls working for you. Let's go outside."

That's really what I'd been waiting for her to say.

The therapist took me outside and had me take the driver's seat in what must have been a 15-year-old Ford. It was fitted with a primitive hand-control system. At the top of the steering wheel was a knob to aid in the turning of the wheel, what we used to call "suicide knobs." I started up the engine and slowly backed out, pushing the lever attached to the steering wheel column. Then I tried to turn the wheel, but it was rough indeed. My football-damaged shoulders are shot. I could barely make it out of the parking lot.

Once however on a straight street, I was fine and did manage to go from one block to another despite the blaring of horns behind me.

"You're doing well," said the therapist. "Now turn into the next driveway you see, then back out into the street."

The driveway had a slight slope to it. I found I was fighting the wheel, with very little effect. That incline might as well have been Mount Everest. The old Ford seemed like it had no power steering at all. Moreover, my shoulders began to ache as I twisted and turned my body trying to maneuver the car wheel. To top it off, my bum knee began to throb because the rod attached to the steering post had pushed my leg into a cramped position. It was almost impossible for me to coordinate the pushing of the control stick while at the same time using my left hand to turn the suicide knob.

The jig was up, and I knew it. But the examiner seemed determined to show that she'd given me a fair shake. "Let's give it one more try. We'll get on a highway for a bit."

Was there still a chance that she'd certify me? No, not after the ensuing 15-minute stretch of on- and off-ramps alive with cars speeding around 60-70 mph while I tried to coordinate the pushing and pulling of the levers. I was very glad to finally drive into the parking spot reserved for this torture machine.

"Well," said my cheery therapist when I had brought the car to rest and returned the key to her. "How did you like it?"

My body had failed me, and she knew it. I said, "Let's go upstairs and do the paperwork."

"At least, you gave it a good try, Mr. Ballard."

Ten minutes later, I was signing a paper giving up my right to operate an automobile under any conditions. The therapist said, "Usually, I go through a checklist of various kinds of limitations that might be placed on your license— local shopping, only in daylight, restricted to church, but in your case, you're totally grounded."

"Totally."

"Yes."

She reached over to her desk and handed me a paper with a list of senior-citizen riding services for Saratoga County. And indeed, there were provisions for transportation to the senior center, the YMCA, shopping and medical appointments. The only catch was the need to schedule the appointments well in advance.

"Are you going to report this to the DMV?"

Surprisingly, she said "No." Only my doctor would be informed, and it would be up to him to decide on a proper course of action.

My internist of 30 years, was about as good a friend to me as a physician can be without losing his professional objectivity. He'd seen me through and orchestrated all my operations and had definitely been there when I had a bout with prostate cancer that was cured by cryosurgery back in the early '90s when I was the eighth person in the world to undergo that procedure.

He was a Philadelphian, and he'd spent a year at my high school before his pharmacist dad had moved the family to Atlantic City. We shared a love of photography and Philly cheesesteak sandwiches.

He brought out the report. "That's the end, old buddy. I need your word that you won't drive anymore." He glanced again at the paper. It was full of negative checkmarks. "There's no need for me to report this to the DMV,

so you can keep your license for identification purposes."

Curious about my exact status, and his duties in that regard, I later checked the New York DMV site. It became very clear that I was, in fact, now officially forbidden to drive, bound by my self-knowledge of my infirmity and his command to me. Were I to drive a car and be in an accident, I would have committed a felony. My doctor, according to the way I read the DMV instructions, was not legally bound to report me to the DMV, but the American Medical Association states that the physician should use his "best judgment" in such situations. Just six states require a physician to report physically or mentally impaired drivers.

Had my doctor written such a letter, it would have set off a lengthy process whereby I would have been called before a DMV examiner and been forced to undergo a complete re-examination as if I were a 16–year-old applying for a license. And any misstep along the way—a parking ticket, a speeding violation, would have immediately resulted in the full suspension of my license.

National practices vary in this respect, with 32 states having age-related requirements for license renewal. Some, like California, require drivers, over age 70, to take a written exam test. But a look at the various laws shows a mix of driving-cessation legislation. Most have settled on a pattern of setting a cutoff age, 65-70, at which time a driver must renew his license in person rather than by mail, and that license is set for a time period, usually half the time of a person under that age.

Moreover, the senior driver sometimes is required to have an eye test at that session, which gives the motor vehicle staff the ability to assess the physical condition of the applicant. States also have varying standards for who can report the need for a driver to be re-evaluated, with some of them actually making it possible for a bystander to report the impaired condition of a driver.

This is a serious business indeed. Back in 2003, an 86-year-old California man plowed into a summer farmers' market, killing 10 people and wounding 63, his car, at times, reaching speeds of 60 mph. He claimed "pedal error" as an excuse. He was found guilty of vehicular homicide but was let off by the judge at sentencing because of age and illness.

As with gun control, there's a solid constituency that makes it almost impossible to pass legislation regulating the driving of senior citizens. Too many of us vote too regularly! New Hampshire had a law requiring those over 75 to take a road test that was revoked in 2011 when an 86-year-old legislator said it smacked of age discrimination. The same thing happened with a Washington, D.C., law of similar ilk. However, studies of these various state interventions show mixed results in terms of reducing accidents among seniors.

I gave my word to my internist, walked out of the office and got into my car, now piloted by my girlfriend. I asked her to take me to Dunkin' Donuts so I could have my favorite—a glazed donut and an extra-large decaffeinated coffee.

Chapter 5
They Took the Car Keys Away. What Now?

It's a sad feeling, being deprived of your car. Even a trip to the bank to cash a check becomes a project. But it's the long trips, the rides down winding mountain roads, the thrill of being one with a car as it negotiates curves, and the pure joy of accelerating out of an off-ramp that we car lovers enjoy so much.

Oh, I had so many roads that I loved to navigate, particularly challenges like the Lincoln Drive that borders Philadelphia's Schuylkill River. Here, a series of hairpin turns have killed many a driver and wounded many others, including, tragically, the great Teddy Pendergrass who overturned his Rolls Royce in 1982, resulting in his paralysis from his neck down. Guess I must have traveled that road a thousand times and in each instance was careful going into it—you can never really go slow enough on it to be safe—and happy when I could hit the gas and accelerate out of it! Some Philadelphians now call it "Dead Man's Gulch."

The reader might be getting the idea that I was a real car nut. Well, I was. I really couldn't understand it when one of my colleagues who drove a Toyota Corolla said, "I never could get excited by cars. They're just a means to get from one point to another." Heresy, indeed, in my book.

Among my favorite magazines, for many years were *Road and Track, Car and Driver* and *Automobile*. Yes, I knew all of the g-forces—the cornering-speed measurement for practically every automobile that counted—and could compare their 0-60 speeds. I would spend hours reading over the incredibly beautiful brochures, now long since gone, that detailed all the alluring features of an automobile: power windows, leather seats, number of gears, sunroof, you name it. I knew cars backward and forward.

For most of my life, I only drove stick-shift cars, everything from a new Volvo 122S to a six-year-old BMW 540i. I can't imagine, even at age 87, why I was like that. An old girlfriend said to me one morning as I perused the New York Times automobile section—"Why do you want to do that? You've already got a good one."

She put her arm on my shoulder. "Are you sad about something?" Indeed, I was. It was like I'd buy one car, research it thoroughly, and then, once I had it, find some fault with it— not enough speed, drove like a marshmallow, didn't corner well, hurt my back after a long drive, mileage was lousy. Whatever the car was, I'd definitely find its weakness, and then be free to experience once again the joy of the hunt.

I can't begin to say how negatively this affected my finances over the years. But sometimes, to my own surprise, I'd make a wise economic move such as when I purchased an old Buick Electra station wagon that had 135,000 miles on it and drove it to 245,000 miles. But mostly, I was just plain never satisfied.

Sad to say, this compulsion extended to sailboats and cameras, with dire financial results. But of those, another story, another time. Did I enjoy them? Sure. It was like Christmas every time I bought a new car.

My auto mechanics became almost as important to me as my doctors. I'll never forget one. His name was Tim Smith. He'd worked in Albany for a Mercedes dealership and then set up his own shop in a small garage in the city's South End. Tim was a minimalist and a true philosopher who looked with scorn on the coming electronics boom. His forte was old Mercedes, the older, the better.

He truly loved my circa-1985 European model year Mercedes 500 SEC coupe that had 80,000 miles on it when I purchased it. Tim was the only person in Albany who would work on it. The dealers shunned it. If Tim could find a used part to repair your car, he'd do so. His prices were fair and often brought an unexpected smile to a worried customer's face when they were presented with a $150 bill for a repair that would have cost $500 at a dealership.

The performance of my 500 SEC was outstanding on the road that most determined for me the capability of a car. It was a winding stretch of hills and curves that ran for 10 miles along the upper part of Lake George. It was bordered by trees all the way, and at the very bottom of the descent, one was greeted with a pictorial prize: a panoramic view of the great Lake George, cupped by mountains.

Never once did this vista fail to bring joy to my heart, and still today, each time I see it, I say, "Hello, Lake!" That, in turn, inevitably brings to my mind, the beautiful Sunday-evening recital of Otis Tucker, a chef and concert singer, who at Lake George's Silver Bay resort sang "Then You'll Remember Me," and the sound poured out over the pristine silver calm of the lake.

My dad, as the reader might gather, was not the most encouraging of persons and, particularly, didn't think much of my driving or of my mechanical ability. When I did drive, he was always on me about my perceived ignoring of the instrument panel: "Look at your gauges. You just get in a car,

put in the key and drive away. Look at the needles!"

But Dad did love his cars, as did the uncle who raised me till I went to live with my father at age 14. His first post-war car was a 1947 Ford, and it was a beautiful black color. When I was home from college in the summer, he would make me wash it every week, coming out every 15 minutes to see how the job was going. First, it had to be washed down with a hose—no rags involved, just the hose. Then I had to bring out a bucket of soapy water and scrub down the entire car with a towel. Next a good rinsing with the hose set to high pressure. Finally, a drying with a clean towel to be followed by polishing the car with a chamois cloth. Not a single white smudge was to be left. This ritual had to be done by me every Saturday morning if I was in town. His last car before he died was a 1958 Pontiac Bonneville. It was a beauty, although difficult for me to maneuver into and out of the garage. As you can imagine, I didn't want to put a scratch on it.

I guess it was because of my dad's criticism that the first thing I did upon getting a job in New York was to buy a model automobile engine kit. It must have had 150 pieces, and I put it together piece by piece: valves, cylinder heads, transmission. When I finished, I knew exactly how an engine worked. Unfortunately, my dad never saw the finished product. He died a few months before I finished it.

My own first car was a Plymouth sedan. I bought it in 1961. I think it was about 10 years old, a real wreck, totally suited to New York City. Nobody was going to steal that jalopy, believe me! By then I was living on Manhattan's Upper West Side in a beautiful third-floor walk-up on West 103rd Street off Riverside Drive. I'd just taken my first teaching job as an assistant professor of political science at the City College of New York. It was a brownstone, owned by a wonderful lady by the name of Mrs. Frumkin. Below me on the second floor was a couple who were to be my dear friends until death took them both away.

The woman's name was Dell. She was a Puerto Rican dressmaker whose skills were so great that she could afford her own studio in midtown Manhattan. Her dresses were things of beauty and much sought-after by her mostly wealthy white clientele. She was also a great cook, with Caribbean jambalaya her primary specialty.

Her husband, Jose Hayles, became like an uncle to me. What can I tell you of Jose? Panamanian, he had been trained as a dentist, but by some set of circumstances had stopped practicing, then worked as a laborer around the Caribbean during World War II. He was to be by my side as I went through all the pangs of ownership of that Plymouth, which broke down a lot at first but then became more reliable. He loved to help me through the things that come along with car ownership. He taught me how to change oil on a Manhattan street, repair tires, put snow tires on a car. During the summers, we'd spend hours just sitting on the fenders of the car and chatting with the neighbors.

I remember still the cars that framed the years of my young adulthood. I turned in the Plymouth and purchased a used, maybe three-year-old American Rambler. I kept that for a few years, then got married, and that definitely changed my life.

For then, in rapid succession, came a series of automobiles. I can barely count them now, but there was a Peugeot 504, a lovely, beautifully designed French car that had an aversion to starting in cold weather and a rather nasty tendency to wash out when going around a curve, and finally, just before my divorce, a Volvo 122S, my first totally new car. I don't remember the reason for its departure, but I suspect it was related to myriad troubles with its carburetor and radiator. I just lost faith in it. Plus, there was the not-so-small matter of the financial consequences of the divorce.

Then, amidst all the turmoil of the '60s, I came upon an ad for a 10-year-old Mercedes 250S, supposedly babied by its owner. Still determined to find a perfect vehicle for a cheap price, I called upon the services of a fellow who named himself the "Lemon Buster." An experienced mechanic, he promised to come with his bag of tools and evaluate a car before you purchased it.

He met me at the home of the auto's owner, then proceeded to check out the carburetor, distributer, rotors, spark plugs and cylinder pressure before declaring the car perfect. After charging me $50 for his services, he gave me a certificate attesting to the "excellent" condition of the vehicle.

After checking the towing capacity of the Benz, I put a hitch on it and set about towing my first boat, a small used 16-foot sailboat. As I drove north on the New Jersey Turnpike, within five miles, I heard a clunking sound in the back of the car.

At first, I couldn't believe the noise. I figured something was loose in the boat. I pulled over at the next rest stop, checked out the interior of the boat and the trailer connections, saw nothing, and started up again.

The sound worsened, and I had to pull off the road. The weight of the hitch had literally destroyed the back end of the Benz and the differential. The repair cost was astronomical. I ended up junking the car. All I had wanted to do was to buy one car that would last me the rest of my life. But, as old sailors say, "It's an ill wind that blows no good." Down the road, another car awaited me.

Chapter 6
Maybe a Motor Scooter Can Replace My Car?

A few days after my failed exam at Sunnyview, I began to ponder my alternatives for transportation. I really didn't like the idea of taking the bus to hang out at the senior citizens' center. I felt the need for mobility of some sort. Then it hit me.

Years ago, while I was in the Army in France, my best buddy, Forest Hansen, bought a Lambretta motor scooter. Along with the similar Vespa scooter, it competed for the European mass transportation market in the aftermath of World War II. Vespa sales soared when Audrey Hepburn and Gregory Peck took a scooter joyride—you can always catch it on YouTube—in the 1953 hit movie, "Roman Holiday."

When I was offered an opportunity to visit my girlfriend who was an au pair on a farm in the south of France, Hans offered me the use of his Lambretta to get there. That was a real act of generosity on the part of a friend, particularly since I'd never used a scooter before. It was summer, and the distance from Paris to my destination was about a three-day's travel by scooter. This was in 1955, and I was an enlisted man at SHAPE headquarters in Paris.

With a *Guide Michelin* in my scooter pack, I took off on a beautiful morning and began my ride through the French countryside. I'd plotted out my trip pretty thoroughly, scheduling lunch stops where I'd have a ham and cheese sandwich, then hit the road till evening when I would stop at a country inn.

There, of course, things became different. I would order a half-liter carafe of the house wine, have pâté as an appetizer, then enjoy the specialty of the house. In those days, these inns cooked only one dish for the day, and what a treat that was! I remember the succulent meats, the fresh tomato sauces, bread still warm from the oven and plates heaped full of *haricots verts* and roasted potatoes. Man, did I ever eat well!

Ten years after the war's end, the roads were bare of automobiles. I had sweeping views of the mountains, valleys and rivers of the French countryside. The innkeepers were hospitable, the women beautiful in their peasant smocks.

I arrived at my destination, a farm high in the mountains, perched above a mist-covered valley. I spent the time with my girlfriend and the two tots under her charge, the owners having been made aware that I would be there. After a week, I mounted the Lambretta and headed back to Paris.

Twenty miles outside of the farm, I felt a twinge in my right calf. I didn't pay it much attention. I just continued on, ate a delicious supper and went to sleep.

In the morning, I couldn't get out of bed. The small ache had turned into a huge pain, and my leg was swollen up something awful. A phone call brought the innkeeper to my room. He took one look at the leg and said he'd call a doctor. That was fine, except now I only had three days left on my leave.

The doctor arrived and in short order diagnosed my condition as gout, probably brought on, said he, by my overindulgence in wines on the trip and the cramped driving position on the Lambretta. He gave me medicine but said I definitely wouldn't be able to drive the scooter back to Paris. I'd have to take a train.

I was in a real fix. The nearest American base was 20 miles away, and if I reported in sick, I would probably be permanently reassigned there, losing my admittedly privileged position at SHAPE headquarters in Paris. I'd be down in the boondocks until my enlistment was up in September. And what was to be done with Hans' Lambretta?

Well, folks, the U.S. Army doesn't leave anyone behind. By hook or crook, the Lambretta was shipped back to Paris, I received a train ticket, and in four days, Corporal Ballard was resting well in his bunk back at Supreme Headquarters Allied Powers Europe. Hans' Lambretta was back in one piece, and so was I.

Over half a century later, I thought: a Lambretta. That would be the ticket! Alas, there was no dealer nearby, but I went on the web and located a Vespa store in the Albany area, determined— after my exam failure—to have a set of wheels, one way or another. The shop was a few minutes away, and once inside, my friend Fred and I were greeted with rows of gleaming Vespa motorbikes. Fred had been my staunch sailing buddy over the past 27 years. Now he was chauffeuring me around as I searched for a car substitute.

Earlier that week, I had inquired of my Sunnyview examiner if I could legally operate a scooter because driving it required a valid license. Acknowledging that I'd passed all the mental and reflex parts of the exam, she replied that it would be fine if I was able to pass a DMV motor-scooter safety course.

The Vespa could be controlled completely by hand, something that I could manage easily. There was one small problem: At every stop, my bum right leg, the numb one that couldn't tell the difference between an accelerator and a brake, would have to

support my body weight and that of the scooter. I'd have to test it now.

With the support stand off, I mounted a scooter with Fred holding onto one side of it and the salesman the other.

"Hey, mister, you got to hold it upright," the latter said, as my right leg almost collapsed under the Vespa's weight. Seemed like motor scooters had put on a few pounds since 1955.

Well, the standard two-wheel model was definitely out of the question, but there was one more possibility. The Piaggio MP3. It sat in the back of the shop and looked to be my salvation. Neither scooter nor motorcycle, the MP3 is a mechanical wonder. It has three wheels, one in the rear and a coupled two-wheel independent suspension setup in the front.

This vehicle, while capable of leaning up to 40 degrees when cornering, can also maintain a perfectly upright stable position with no corresponding need for the driver to put their feet on the ground when coming to a stop. At rest at a red light or stop sign, the machine also has a front-wheel locking function that stabilizes it in a vertical or moderately leaning position. Theoretically, a driver could go all day long without ever having to prop up the vehicle with their legs, as would be the case with a motorcycle or scooter. And once home, the driver could just climb off this oddly shaped 600-pound vehicle and walk away from it.

Even without the use of its midship-mounted parking stand, the trike would remain upright. Capable of speeds up to 80 mph and averaging 55 miles a gallon of gas, the MP3 stood out to me as an appealing alternative to a car, particularly since it also has lots of cargo space under the rear seat. Indeed, right here in the United States, back in 2008, a couple of adventurous fellows in their 70s took a month-long trip across the country in a pair of MP3's.

No question about it; I had to at least try one out.

"This is your last chance, mister," said the salesman, who had looked skeptically at me from the second I entered the store with my Dolomite walker.

"I appreciate your letting me try." I pushed hard on my cane and somehow

or another, with help from Fred, managed to mount the machine. I grasped the steering wheel and quickly imagined myself cruising around the side streets of my neighborhood.

But it became obvious that the MP3 sat too high for me to mount unassisted, and almost impossible for me to dismount. My arthritic body was simply up too high.

"Hey, you guys," I said, "get me down from here."

They both laughed, and helped by a female clerk, managed my descent from the scooter.

I gathered up what dignity I could, then laughed along with them. "Guess that ends my scooter days." I'd already told them about the time in France, trying to appear as an old, seasoned scooter-hand.

When, a few days later, I told my doctor about my aborted attempt to buy a Vespa, he exploded: "You want me to inform the DMV. Your body's a wreck now, and you'd better get used to that. No more tricks!"

"All right, but you can't really blame a guy for trying, can you?" He opened the office door. "Remember, the DMV's only a mouse click away."

Chapter 7
Comfort Bikes Might Just Be the Ticket!

Where next to turn? Ah, a bicycle, that would get me to the library. And to the main shopping center of my town five miles away.

Fig. 7.1 An Elgin Bluebird, just like mine

I remembered my first real bike, an Elgin Bluebird sold by Sears. I must have been 9-10 years old. It was on a cold, snowless Christmas morning. I came downstairs with my brother to see the Yule tree all lit up and beautifully decorated with silver bulbs and glittering red and yellow lights. Right in front of the tree, sitting on its rear stand, and all covered with tinsel and red ribbons was my brand-new bike. My divorced dad, just having been made a police officer, had bought it for me. I was living with my mom, Aunt Alice and Uncle Jerry, a pharmacist.

Uncle Jerry was in a heavy woolen sweater and was smiling, something he rarely did because his business was failing. After a breakfast of scrambled eggs and bacon, toast, and a hot Ovaltine, I went out to ride my bike around the block and up to the nearby schoolyard. There was no need to worry about traffic. It was the depth of the Depression, and although my uncle had a car, they were far and few between in those days. You could play an entire stickball game in the street and only have it interrupted once in an hour.

So off I pedaled up the street with all of the neighborhood kids coming out to admire the bike and begging for a ride.

"Hey, Junie, didn't I give you half of my Milky Way?"

"Remember the time I found the book you lost?"

"I'll give you my red marble if you let me ride it!"

Some of the older fellows joined in the chorus of suppliants, but my uncle had made it very clear that no one else was to ride the bike.

Finally, tired and cold after an hour or so, I rode back to my house, parked the Bluebird in front and went in to have a good hot cup of Ovaltine. The term may be unfamiliar to some readers, but it tasted just like a hot chocolate malted milkshake. Delicious!

When, in a half hour, I went back outside, my new Elgin was gone.

I ran back into the house. "Uncle Jerry, Uncle Jerry, my bike is gone!"

He dropped the sports page of the Philadelphia Inquirer, leapt out of his chair and was out the door in a flash. "Where'd you leave it?"

"Right there, right where you're standing!"

He looked up and down the street and shouted to one of the first neighbors, alarmed by my shouts, to arrive: "Plink, somebody took Junie's new bike."

Plink, a tall, very dark-skinned, half-blind giant, said, "That's the worst mistake they ever made." Besides being a pharmacist, my uncle was the local numbers banker and Plink was his enforcer. "What the hell could have been on their minds, Doc?"

By now, both my younger brother and I were standing in the driveway, crying. My mom took us both back into the house, said some calming words and made us hot corn muffins and more Ovaltine—it conquered everything.

Well, that was some Christmas morning. My uncle's friends and "employees" scoured the neighborhood to no avail. But about an hour later, my dad arrived with three of four of his newly made friends from the Police Academy, and they too took up the search for that Elgin bike. Across the street from us, the sons of the Italian grocer tagged along with my dad. They must have scoured every possible hiding place within the surrounding three blocks,

My brother and I just sat at the dining room table, crying—the hot drink had worn off. That bike had a beautiful bell, a rack and a headlight.

There'd been a contest between it and the tinsel as to which gleamed the most.

Finally, my dad walked into the house, the bicycle under his arm—he'd been the captain of his Virginia Union football team. "I'm getting you a lock! Use it!" He paused. "And don't ever let anybody except your brother use it."

The winter weather kept both the bike and me indoors until spring. Then I used it a lot, one time even venturing a good 10 miles from home on a Good Friday afternoon when we were home from school.

It was pretty hard to adhere to my dad's commands, particularly when the chief neighborhood bully decided one Saturday afternoon in the school yard that he'd like to take a ride on my bike.

Raymond Bradford, muscled, smooth of face and endowed with great athletic ability, was considered the toughest fellow in the neighborhood. He was two grades above me and lived right up the block in a row house rented by his mom, who was a lovely, warm lady. That day, right after a baseball game in the schoolyard, I went over to mount my bike to go home. It was a bit banged up by now, but still my pride and joy.

Just as I went to swing my leg over the saddle, Raymond came over and put a restraining arm over my shoulder. "Let me try it!"

Four or five of our little gang were standing around.

"Oh, boy, Junie's in for trouble,"

"Raymond gonna ride that bike today!"

"What you gonna do, Junie?"

Raymond had 10 pounds on me and was the most skillful boxer in our age group.

I was scared. I think my voice must have trembled a bit, but I turned to face Raymond. "No," I said.

"Man, let me ride that bike!" He pushed me with both hands in the "let's fight now" motion.

I backed away, still holding onto the bike. "Can't let you do it."

He got a really mean look on his face and shoved me again.

I put up my fists like I'd been taught to do by my boxing mentor, Son Reed. "Can't let you do it."

Then somebody said, "Raymond, Plink will kick your ass if you don't leave

Junie alone. You better forget about that damn bike."

Raymond looked me hard in the eye and shoved me one more time. "Didn't really want to ride that old bike anyhow. My mom's buying me a better one."

Everybody laughed. Raymond shook hands with me and said, "Thought you'd be more scared of me than that."

Now I laughed. "I was, but Son told me to never show it."

***

Given my physical condition at age 87, I needed a bike that I could mount. That's not easy for someone who's had a hip replacement, knee surgery, back surgery with fusion for spinal stenosis and a succession of back and shoulder injections.

But the cycling industry has developed the so–called two-wheel comfort or "crank forward," bike to deal with exactly this kind of situation. Perhaps the best known of these bikes is the female model of the **Electra Townie** bike. The high tubes of the male version make it difficult to mount for most folks in my position.

What are its attributes? Primarily, like the other bikes that I would suggest you look at, the crank of the bike is not directly below your feet as on a regular bike but placed from 7 to 12 inches forward of that position. Thus, the name of "crank forward." It's stretched-out so the rider, in an upright position—a bit old, a bit handicapped— is able to put both feet flat on the ground when the bike comes to a stop. The rider is in a lower position than on a regular bike and feels much safer.

These and other comfort bikes usually come in combination with a step-through frame, whereby the physically impaired can back themselves onto the seat so they are able to pull their legs over the lower tube and move into a proper position to pedal the bike. Some also have a feature known as the drop-down seat. You lower it to mount the bike, then pop the seat back up when you're ready to drive off. Unfortunately, bike dealers often give you a lot of measurements, but almost intentionally seem to leave out the step-through height.

Fig. 7.2 Day-6 bikes ready to go

Raleigh makes the **Detour One**, a comfort bike, but its step-over height is 19 inches. In addition, a bike seldom advertised, but widely known by word of mouth is the series of American designed **Day 6 bikes**, designed and developed in the United States by Kelly Hutson. They have a cult following but, like several other comfort or crank-forward bikes, are not readily available in shops, so you'll have to spend some time online checking out reviews. Of course, if you decide to order a bike without a field trial, you should look very carefully at the return policies before making your purchase.

A premium bike in this category is the well-known **Rans Fusion ST**, a beautifully crafted, American-assembled machine made by one of the pioneer recumbent-bike manufacturers. Expensive at close to $2,000, it comes with a standard 27-speed gearing system that maximizes its hill-climbing ability.

Most of these comfort bikes are equipped with different combinations of speeds. Some, to be avoided in my opinion, only come with one speed and are unsuitable for anything other than fairly level roads. Others have the derailleur sprockets usually seen on regular road bikes—7-, 10-, 27-speed, for example. Many other bikes these days come with totally enclosed multispeed internal hubs—Shimano Nexus 7- or 8-speeds, come to mind. They have tremendous advantages, including the ability to change gears at rest.

Fig. 7.3 Sleek Rans Fusion ST

This is an imperative because if you're old and tired, you probably do not have the strength necessary to start off pedaling from a cold start in mid or high gears. This, unfortunately, can happen with a regular derailleur system if you did not have the foresight to downshift your bike to first gear before you came to a stop—you're just plain stuck out there on the highway. The hubs also don't throw chains off of cogs and, being completely enclosed, are pretty much immune to dust and rain damage.

It's critical that you make a good choice of gearing because due to the forward position of the pedals, it's difficult to stand up on some comfort bikes if you want to pump it up a steep hill. You might just have to get off and walk it up the rest of the way, which could turn out to be a real hassle.

Once you begin exploring bikes, you'll see that the word, "step-through" is relative. A Day 6 bike, for example, is moderately high at 19 inches. So are the Electra Townie and the Rans Fusion ST at 19 inches. They somewhat compensate for that height by having very low seats, which makes them mountable from the rear. In my own case, a negotiable step-through height starts at 15 inches, and that's barely manageable.

Worth your attention is the **Biria Easy Boarding** model with a step-through height below 10 inches. It comes with a seven-speed derailleur system and can be purchased for under $600. Close to it in design and accessibility would be the **Sun Streamway**.

Fig. 7.4 13-50 Sun Streamway

Don't expect any of these bikes to be speed demons. They have higher handlebars, an upright position and

lower seats than regular road bikes. My
own attempt to purchase a comfort
two-wheel bike ended when I went to
my local bike shop to check out the
Townie. Oh, it was beautiful indeed,
but I couldn't mount it. The step-
through height was just too plain high.

Chapter 8
What About a Recumbent Trike?

About 15 years ago, while vacationing up in the Adirondacks, I was whizzing around mountain turns at 45 mph, when I stumbled upon and almost demolished a strange apparition in the road—a guy, in a low-slung recumbent bike, no flag, no lights. He must have been moving along at 20 mph.

I drove on to the resort, and about an hour later who should come driving in, but that fellow, whom I'd already decided was suicidal.

I walked right up to him. "Mister, are you crazy? I almost ran over you back there. How do you expect anybody to stop and see you when they're coming around those hairpin turns?"

Just about then, his wife and daughter walked up to us. They hadn't overheard my remarks. "How was the ride, dear?" his spouse inquired.

"Okay."

I turned to walk away, shaking my head.

He called out after me. "Sorry, mister, maybe you have a point."

I found out later he was the new manager of the resort.

This was the first time I'd ever seen a recumbent bike, and I'd come upon one of their major shortcomings: They're really not that safe on heavily traveled or dangerously configured roads where a car driver might suddenly come around a bend. I was a careful and seasoned driver. Think what might have happened had a teenager in a pickup truck come around that curve.

Nevertheless, stymied by the inaccessibility of what had been touted as a good choice for me and by the absence in my upstate New York town of any shops that stocked other comfort bikes, I decided to take a good look at recumbent trikes. Besides, I'd begun to feel the need for something with three wheels, a tricycle, since my balance was not the greatest and I'd definitely be more stable on three wheels rather than two. And so, I forsook the allure of the comfort bike and entered the wide and challenging world of recumbent bikes and trikes.

So off I was. First of all, there are two categories of recumbent bikes. One is the two-wheeled version. I dismissed it out of hand, though there are indeed some beautiful designs and some physically challenged folks use and enjoy them. On my part, with sundry various lower body ailments, I didn't want to risk being run over by a car or falling flat onto the road because I was unable to lift my legs high enough to engage the pedals and get the traction necessary to start the bike moving and keep it going. In all of this discussion, I'm referring to reasonable solutions for a physically handicapped person.

No, instead you have to direct your attention to the alternative and much safer and more stable, three-wheel recumbent trike, which has become much more popular and now outsells the recumbent two-wheeler by a margin of three to one.

Allow me to reiterate my needs. I wanted to be able to go up to pick up clothes from the cleaners, stop by the Chinese restaurant for lunch, pick up my meds at the local pharmacy and perhaps do local appointments with doctors. All of these services were available within a six-mile radius of my house.

The trike had to have storage space to at least carry light grocery items. Recreationally, I wanted something that could be transported in the back of a car so I could try out some of the excellent local bike paths that run along the Mohawk and the Hudson. And it had to be fun and safe since at my age I wasn't looking to be hospitalized with a busted hip.

Where would I keep the trike? Well, the garage might do in summer. But what to do when the car had to come inside and intrude on the trike's space? Could I defy all order and put it in my living room? What about lights, safety flags and water bottles? Where would they be placed on the trike? What kind of pedals would I need? What kind of drivetrain was required for comfortable riding on nearby trails? Most importantly, would a recumbent trike

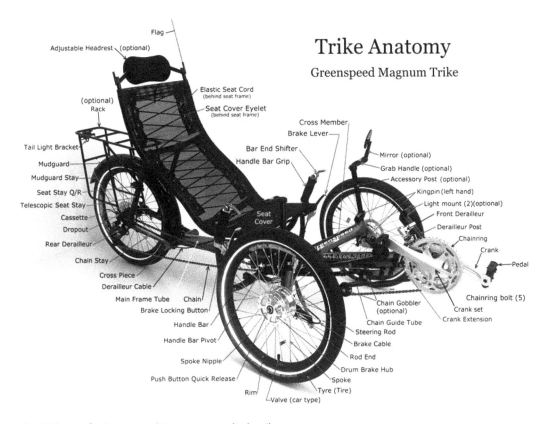

Trike Anatomy
Greenspeed Magnum Trike

Fig 8.1 Parts of a Greenspeed Magnum, a tadpole trike

be safe, given my proximity to a metropolitan area? The seemingly endless questions resulted in months of pleasant research and diversion in a time of national domestic turmoil.

There are two types of recumbent trikes. The first and most popular, the one that you see most often out on a bike path, is called the **Tadpole.** Its distinguishing feature is that it has two wheels forward and is propelled by a single drive-wheel behind. The second type is called the **Delta** trike. It has one wheel forward and is propelled by two wheels in the back. The tadpole, being lower to the ground, is more stable and less easily mounted; the Delta sits higher and is definitely easier indeed to mount.

As with all things today, there is a site that is the center of information about these trikes. It's Bentrideronline.com. Others are Tadpole Rider and Trike Asylum. To be sure, you'll find all of the usual inhabitants there:the opinionated, the

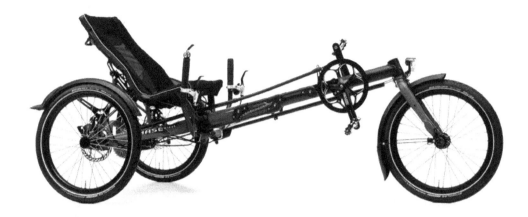

Fig. 8.2 Hass Kettwiesel Allround, A Delta Trike

helpful ones and the "snappers," those who can barely wait to finish their morning coffee before going to the site to ambush the first inquiring reader who makes a mistake on terminology or, in some cases, English grammar!

Let's start with the Delta trikes. A good example of this would be the 90-inch-long, 30-inch-wide **Jouta Delta**, a recent offering by a Dutch company, distributed in the United States by Trident, a pioneering American trike firm. Its width is important because it will fit through most doors. But its long and you'll definitely need to find a good place to keep it.

Its 16-inch seat height is one of its strong points. Most people should be able to mount and dismount it. A trike may look beautiful and have sleek lines, but if it entraps you, what good is it? At 60 pounds, this trike is heavy, which tells you that it's going to be a bear if you want to fit it into your SUV. So you'll probably have to look into a trailer or bike rack if you wish to transport it to a trail.

It's very important that you gauge such factors as a trike's portability. If you're looking to buy one, it's not because of the novelty or that you want to sit low or that you want to be noticed, but, generally, because you can't ride a regular bike anymore and need the exercise or some means of local transportation. And if you have a disability, it may be rough for you to load a heavy trike into a vehicle, onto a rack, or on a trailer.

Delta trikes do have one strong advantage over tadpoles. Their turning circle is a lot tighter, so they are more maneuverable on a trail and, because of their height, you're a lot more likely to be observed by an automobile driver.

The next thing you have to look at in any trike, Delta or tadpole alike, is the BB height, the "bottom bracket height." This is the assembly upon which your pedals are mounted, and its center is an important measuring point. To put it another way, that's where your pedals are.

It's very important that you note this distance and the difference between it and the seat height. Most of these bottom brackets are in the 14-16-inch height, but they can go higher.

If they do, your legs and feet must go higher in the air, thus fighting against the force of gravity in contrast to your stance on a regular bike where your legs and feet are pushing downward.

Fig. 8.3 Bottom bracket is in the center of this crankset

Too big a difference is not good for lots of us with diabetes or numbness problems in the feet. Knee, hernia or ankle ailments could also be aggravated by that situation

There's another hidden problem with the Delta trikes. In the same way that a comfort bike's step-over height could be too high, so is it possible for the boom, or tube, of a Delta trike to sit too high for you to comfortably step over. The seat itself might be the right height to accommodate a partially disabled person, but if you can't lift your legs over the boom, you still can't mount the trike. Some folks seem to solve this problem by rotating the handlebars of the Delta outward. They then sit down and—with the help of their hands—lift their legs over the boom of the Delta trike.

Following in the pattern of regular road bikes, there is an awe-inspiring and truly bewildering number of speeds (gears) available for trikes, both Delta and tadpole. In the case of the Jouta, it starts at seven speeds and then, depending on the configuration of the trike, can have three speeds (cranks) up front and seven cogs on the back-wheel derailleur making for a very common 21 speeds overall. This should give most riders the ability to manage most hills.

Some trikes can have as many as thirty speeds, causing confusion and uncertainty to those of us of an age to remember when a 10-speed bike was considered top of the line. More recently, two- or three-speed cranksets have sometimes been supplanted by either a Patterson Metropolis drive or the more expensive Schlumpf drive.

Either of these additions to a trike makes it possible now for a rider to shift down to a lower gear when the trike isn't moving. Thus, as pointed out before, if you forget to shift down, you're not left with the terrible problem of having to start from a high gear. More than that, they rid the

crankshaft of chain rings and cables, giving a cleaner look to the BB.

Commonly, Delta and tadpole trikes can be found with the following internal hubs: a Nexus 8-speed; a Nu Vinci N380, and a Rohloff 14-speed. The latter is the most expensive and seemingly the choice of riders with deep pockets. Again, all of the above hubs give the rider the opportunity to start from scratch or change gears without being in motion.

Fig. 8.4 An internal hub, a Rohloff mounted on a Greenspeed Trike

Fig. 8.5 A typical 3-ring crankshaft

Fig. 8.6 A typical bike cassette

Fig. 8.7 A bar end shifter and brake mechanism

On the web, there are ongoing disputes about the regular derailleur vs. these internal hubs, but such arguments almost uniformly come out in favor of the latter, particularly since the chains don't jump off of them as they do with a regular wheel. That's important for physically impaired folks who definitely don't want to be dealing with such a problem while enjoying the view of a beautiful fall sunset.

How is the returning rider to approach the problem of selecting a proper drive train for their trike? There's a simple solution indeed. It's called "count the gear inches." Unless one has a good week or so of study time, you can go nuts trying to figure out the varying configurations of gear combinations needed to 1. Get you up a steep hill; 2. Keep you moving at a steady pace on flat terrain; 3. Permit you to keep peddling going down a steep hill. That's what you need to know to start, but for those who wish to explore this subject more in depth, I've prepared a short introduction to gearing matters in an appendix.

Like all things, the "gear inches" number will vary with cost. Thus, the **TerraTrike** basic model, **the Rover** in its 8 speed configuration will have a gear inches range of 24-66 for 42 gear inches while its most expensive model, the X-30 speed Rambler has a gear range of 18-90 or 72 gear inches. The **Greenspeed Magnum**, a more expensive trike, in its basic configuration would have a gear speed of 18-95, or 77 gear inches, about par for a mid-upper range trike. The lower the number, the steeper the hill that can be climbed, the higher the number, the faster you can pedal downhill. *Et voila*, mystery solved. As to how to actually shift the gears, there are excellent tutorials to be found on manufacturers' sites and on YouTube.

Now back to the Jouta. It comes in two configurations—with or without a differential in the back. Most Delta trikes seem to come with only the right wheel being driven by the chain, thus, causing the rider to have an ongoing struggle to compensate for the tendency of the trike to move to the right. This may cause a crab-wise motion and a lifting of the front wheel when you're going up a very steep hill.

The Jouta will add a differential for about $150 to its base price. But any Delta will track better and more smoothly with it.

Even riding relatively high on a Delta trike, it's important that the new rider either purchase a pair of so-called "clipless" shoes or Power Grip retainers to guarantee that your feet will stay attached to the pedals. Clipless shoes are indeed a misnomer, so-named to differentiate them from earlier times when bike riders actually put their shoes into toe clips.

Paradoxically, clipless shoes do have small metal clips on their bottom, which lock into holes set for them on the appropriate matching pedal. They are your primary guard against "leg suck," a horrible event which ensues when your foot slips off of a recumbent trike pedal and your backward moving limbs are run over by the rear wheel and chassis or wheels of your trike. It can be very traumatic.

The Jouta trike is a new entry in the Delta field, but the **Greenspeed Anura**, designed by the legendary Australian recumbent pioneer, Ian Sims, is better known and well established. Priced in the upper 20s in its base configuration, the Anura, with a standard differential, competes with the German-built and much more expensive but highly regarded, **Hase Kettweisel**. The latter, in a suspended and differential equipped version, can easily cost over $6,000. Again, the differential can add up to $700 to the price of a Delta trike, but it's worth it.

An alternative to any of these three Delta trikes would be a **Sun Seeker Delta** trike. Hase, in an attempt to broaden its market presence, recently introduced a much cheaper Delta trike,

the Trigo, which is distinguished by its relatively low price ($2,500), its high seat height (23-26 inches) and the option of purchasing it with either traditional underseat Delta steering or the more familiar upright handle bars.

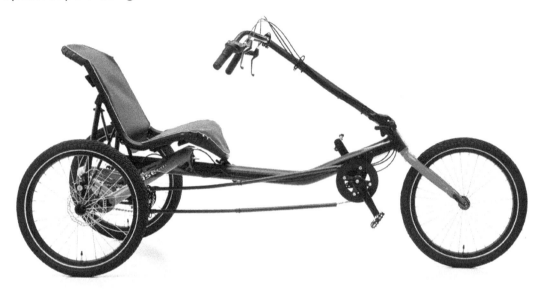

Fig. 8.8 Hase Trigo with upright steering

Fig. 8.9 Hase Trigo with underseat steering

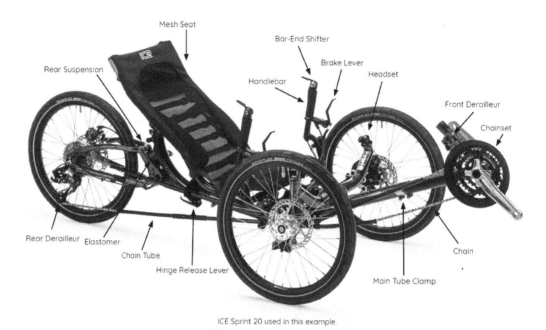

Fig. 8.10 Parts of an Ice Sprint

Now let's take a look at the tadpoles. As noted earlier, these are characterized by having two wheels forward and one wheel behind. There's no need for a differential, as there is only one driven wheel in the back. You immediately have the advantage that the wheels up front are less likely to skitter from side to side in a climbing situation.

Tadpoles come either with underseat steering where the handles emerge from beneath the seat and indirectly control the turning of the wheels through linkages, or direct steering, much as with a regular bike, where the handles are directly attached to the kingpins, with no intermediary linkage. Most higher-end trikes have the more sophisticated underseat steering that generally has a lighter feel than the direct, above-seat steering. But Catrike, a prime American manufacturer, has stuck with the direct steering and has legions of happy followers.

Many tadpoles, catering to customers eager for speedy and thrilling rides, are low-slung to the ground, some as low as six inches. But if my visual assessment of the age and physical condition of the audience at a recent trade fair is correct, the main buyers of recumbent trikes are a bit weight-challenged, somewhat physically impaired and pushing age 60 or older. As the saying goes, "They're not spring chickens." Few of them, in my opinion, are going to be happy about lifting their bodies upward against the force of gravity of a seat in a recumbent trike that sits exactly six inches off the ground. Or, as is more frequently the case, 10-13 inches off the ground. For the physically handicapped among us, it's difficult to sit down in these trikes and almost impossible—with aches in your back, knees and hips—to get out of them. You need a fire truck to lift you out. For reference, the average height of a dining room chair is 17-18 inches.

It seems that the early pitch of trike development was toward performance and trying to keep up with the two-wheelers. A look at the sites confirms this because the enthusiasts like to boast about "the recumbent smile" and "blasting around curves." Younger riders can routinely hit an average of 15 mph and on a downhill run, maybe 30 mph. It's definitely true that the higher the seat, the less stable the trike and the more susceptible it is to tipping at speed. The designers are trapped by the laws of nature.

Recumbent trikes, on the other hand, are more comfortable than an upright bike because your body is cushioned, as some say, in a "recliner on wheels." It can be made even more comfortable when equipped with special balloon tires or with suspension systems. The latter are pricey, but universally praised add-on options that can shoot the cost of a trike up above $3,500.

Tadpole users frequently talk of taking 30-mile-a-day cruises, from which they emerge painless and ready to sit down for an evening drink and a good meal. Their buttocks are spared from the pain inflicted by hard regular bicycle seats. Some say you can ride for hours in them and not feel any back pain.

There's much to be said about riding through the countryside, admiring nature as you go along, and then, being able to stop and take a nap, if need be, right in your trike. It's a great touring vehicle if one sticks to the many bike trails that festoon the country. The internet is full of tales of riders who have gone cross-country in their trikes. If I were in better physical shape, I might do it myself.

Fig. 8.11 Faraway places!

What about the safety of these trikes? Imagine now, there you are, low-slung to the ground, riding along a busy city street. Common sense would tell you that you're a sitting duck because it's very hard for a driver to see you, and for you to see the driver. That's pretty clear, and why you don't seem to find any of the manufacturers even recommending that you venture with your trike into rush-hour traffic in a cosmopolitan area.

Rather, there seem to be gentle hints that the trikes are best used on paths or on lightly traveled suburban roads. Nevertheless, trikes are

routinely used in Europe for commuting and sometimes here, too, in the United States.

How safe are recumbent trikes? Well, one commenter on BentRiderOnline said, "Riding down low definitely gives you a new perspective on car/truck bumpers! But in my experience cars will give a bent—even a very low one— more room than an upright. "Almost uniformly, trike riders say that they are more visible than regular bikes and that drivers go out of the way to avoid them. Some think that motorists look upon them as disabled or crazy or both!

Suffice it to say, necessity is the mother of inventions and practically every trike rider equips his vehicle with a large visibility flag, and sometimes with flashing front and rear lights. One particularly popular flag is the Purple Sky Flag sold by TerraCycle. My advice would be that's it's best to hook up with a dealership-sponsored riding club if you want to do long Saturday morning rides. There's safety in numbers.

Trikes are expensive compared to regular road bikes. You can go out and buy a perfectly good bike for about

$500, but even the lowest priced trike is going to cost you a good $1,500. A middle-level trike would cost $2,500-$3,500, and a deluxe, fully suspended model, the equivalent of a Mercedes, can easily top $6,000.

There's no way around this, except by hovering over Craigslist, BentRider.com and eBay. In fact, you can find a good used trike, depending on age and condition, for about two-thirds of the price of a new one. Just looking right now on Craigslist, there are several such sales.

But buying a used trike is also a risk because many of the folks who buy them are weight-challenged and may have put a lot of wear and tear on the chassis and drivetrain of the trike. And once you have purchased the trike, you might have a problem finding a reliable local dealer to repair it, although any good bike mechanic should be able to service it.

So how should you go about purchasing a trike? Recumbent sales in the 2005-12 period were minuscule, less than two percent of total bike sales, which might explain why easily accessible dedicated trike stores are few and far between. The shops that

do exist are often located away from populated areas, causing customers to travel a long distance to try out a trike

Yet a constant refrain on enthusiast sites is the advice to try it before you buy it. To which there's often this response: "But the nearest place is two hundred miles away." That said, if at all possible the consensus is that you should purchase a trike from a brick-and-mortar dealership. You'll be face to face with an expert who can evaluate your needs and point the way to a suitable trike. Moreover, you'll actually be able to ride one for an extended period, maybe an hour or so, to see if you really like it.

You'll also be able to try out several different brands and find a model that is best for your height and weight. Ideally, a trike's boom should be personally fitted to you on the basis of your "X-seam," a special measurement from your butt to the bottom of your feet when you are seated at an angle 10-13 inches from a wall, as would be the case were you to be reclined in a trike.

It's an important measurement. If not properly done, you may develop severe knee, ankle or foot problems when pedaling your new trike. Absent physical access to a trike shop, you'll have to make your purchase online. There are lots of reliable sites to do so, most of which are listed on the Bentrideronline.com.

Tadpoles are not particularly friendly for loading on a rear or front basket because their shape makes that difficult. But most of them have racks, to which can be attached pannier bags for carrying your items. You can't carry much more on the back of a trike than you can on a regular bike, although many folks have indeed set them up for camp touring, mainly trying to follow regular bike trails.

Make seat height a primary focus before you purchase your first trike. The normal seat height for most trikes tends to be 10 inches or below for performance models, 10-13 inches for touring models, and 14 inches and above for those manufactured by companies that made it their business to provide trikes for physically handicapped senior citizens like you and me.

If you're arthritically challenged, forget about those that are 13 and below. One morning a strapping fellow, a personal trainer by profession and an aficionado of recumbent trikes who owned no less than six of them (yes, you can accumulate them just like watches, cars, boats and cameras) drove up to my house with one such trike he was looking to unload.

It was a sight to behold, with fluorescent pedals and beautifully painted manufacturer's lettering. This fellow was about as enthusiastic a salesman, as I've ever met, extolling the virtues of his vehicle and sizing me up in one moment as I came down the driveway leaning on my walker.

"This was made just for you," he said, "You'll look great driving it."

This particular model stood 10 inches off the ground and looked like a go-cart. First, I had to figure out how to sit down in it. That wasn't easy. Remember, I have spinal stenosis.

I couldn't just step over the boom. I had to maneuver myself with my cane to the front of the trike, then gradually back myself over the boom toward the seat, kind of like mounting a horse from the front backward. There's always a crossbar of some sort right in front of the seat. If it's out too far, it's difficult to back all the way to the seat. You have to feel your way with the back of your thighs, then gently ease yourself down. If the two front wheels don't have fenders, after activating the parking brake, you can reach down, grasp them with both hands and let yourself gradually back into the seat.

Once there, I leaned back and felt really good. It was definitely like a recliner. But it also felt like I was in a wheelchair. I felt low, very low, to the ground, which made me a bit fearful.

My new friend told me to put my feet on the pedals. They fit perfectly, but already I had a funny feeling. My legs were jutting upward and outward to reach the pedals. The bottom bracket on this particular trike was a whopping 6½ inches above the seat. I really felt it in my thighs, and especially in the area of the hernia operation, I'd had a year before. Now, to be fair, I only had my sneakers on; clipless shoes would have made my attachment to the pedals feel more secure. But it is a strange feeling when the lower appendages are fighting against the forces of gravity.

Nevertheless, I started pedaling and was amazed at how fast this seven-speed internal hub bike went. I rode around the block three times. My close-by neighbors, retired and therefore home at this morning hour, looked on in astonishment. They'd never seen anything like it.

Then came the reckoning. I had to get up from the seat. And try as I might, I couldn't do it. My legs were just not strong enough. Finally, after maneuvering close to a wooden mailbox post and grasping it, my combined efforts with that of the hulking 200-pounder enabled me to lift myself out of the trike.

He shook his head. "Mister, I wouldn't sell you this trike even if you wanted to buy it. You need something higher."

As a matter of fact, I had tried something higher—the **TerraTrike Rover**, probably the best-selling trike in the country. It's an entry-level trike whose seat height at 16½ inches makes it easily accessible to its target audience: folks who can't ride regular bikes anymore but want to get outside, lose weight and see the birds and the trees.

It's slow, less maneuverable and heavier than more expensive trikes, but owners swear by it. The focus is on usability. It's no accident that TerraTrike is a leader in manufacturing so-called "helper bars" that attach to the trike and aid the rider in entering and exiting.

TerraTrike has an active forum. Its website is a rich resource for all kinds of information on trikes. The company has a sterling reputation, as do practically all of the other trike manufacturers. Indeed, a manufacturer could not long survive were it to do otherwise because the market is so small and the customer base so concentrated and knowledgeable. The seat height of 16½ inches and a BB height of 13 inches are outstanding virtues of the Rover. Your feet and legs are pointed down, not up. That's a far more natural position than is found on most other trikes.

Though coming in at close to a $1,000, a Rover will want to be equipped with a few accessories. I'll go into them here because they are likely to be added to any trike you order. First, come fenders. They'll add $150. Second is a rear rack. Without it, you can't carry anything. It will run you another $75. You might add special retaining straps for the pedals to keep

your feet from slipping off as well as helper bars; bottle holders and water bottles; flags for visibility; and lights, fore and aft. All in all, this beginning trike will run you close to $2,000. And that's in its basic gear configuration. Add on a high-level continuously variable internal hub for your trike, the Nu Vinci N380, and your new kit will cost close to $2,500.

Competing with TerraTrike for entry-level trikes is the American-based Trident firm that makes a very good trike, **the Spike**. In its cheapest configuration, it sells for under $1,000, elevates in price depending primarily on the drivetrain and tops out at $2,500 for an electric-assist model.

The **Sunseeker Eco** is another entry-level trike with a decent price. It has a whopping seat height of 17-18 inches and a BB height of 13½ inches, making it one of the easiest trikes to mount for disabled folks.

Catrike is a highly regarded midlevel American trike firm known for the quality of its paint jobs. One of its most popular models is **the Villager**, a touring trike. But its seat height is only 12½ inches, and the BB height is close to 17 inches. Such a close differentiation might cause a problem for those who might suffer from diabetes or from neuropathy in the foot. Some folks do complain about numbness in their feet after a long time on a trike. "The basic cause of foot numbness on recumbents for many is a bottom bracket higher than the seat," one commenter posted on the BentRider site. But Catrike's reputation is stellar indeed, and the Villager is definitely worth a good look-see and tryout. It, too, like most other trikes can be equipped with helper bars.

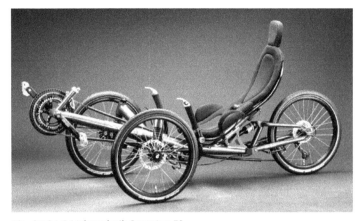

Fig. 8.12 HP Velotechnik Scorpion FS

Fig. 8.13 Ice Adventure FS

Generally priced above the Catrikes are the British-built **Ice trikes**, the Australian-made **Greenspeed series** and the German-manufactured **HP Velotechnik** trikes.

These are top-of-the-line machines, distinguished by meticulous construction, high-grade components, lighter materials and fine design.

An important dividing line amongst trikes lies in their ability or inability to be transported. You will definitely have to search the web for information on this front. Of the Rover, for instance, some enthusiasts say they are able to load it into the back, say, of their RAV4. They fold down the rear seats and place the front wheel of the trike in the space between the front seats. Obviously, this kind of a solution depends on the location of your automatic transmission. But by and large, by hook and crook, maybe catty-corner, most bent riders seem to fit them into the back of their SUVs. But a full-grown trike is definitely not going to fit in the back seat or trunk of your average sedan.

Purchasing a folding trike is one solution to the portability problem. Foldability is found in abundance in the more expensive trikes—the Australian Greenspeeds, the British Ice series, the German HP Velotechnik, the Czech Azub, and in certain entry-level models like the Trident Spike and Stowaway,

the TerraTrike Traveler and the Catrike Dumont and 559.

Some obviously fold easier than others and even then, weighing in at 40 pounds or so, the folded trike can be tough for a senior citizen to load into a SUV or van. Happily, if you Google the name of the folding trike, you probably will be able to see a demonstration of its features on YouTube to help you make a reasoned choice.

Fig. 8.14 Greenspeed Magnum in half-folded position

If your trike can't fold and won't fit comfortably into your vehicle, hitch-mounted carriers are available for purchase on the internet. TerraTrike even has a car-topping kit, and you can always buy a small trailer. But, if like me, you've been through the process of loading bikes on hitches and are physically handicapped, you might well want to limit your selection to a folding trike.

When all is said and done, there is one more aspect of a trike that markedly changes the price, and that is whether it is suspended or not. Now the trike can be only a rear suspension (**the Scorpion FX,** for example) or a full suspension (**Scorpion FS, ICE Adventure FS, Catrike Dumont, Revolution Defiance**). This definitely seems to be a desirable aspect of a trike for those with back and hip problems. But it adds considerably to its cost and weight. Greenspeed, in its Magnum model, depends more on its engineering and a special selection of tires to give their trike better cushioning.

At this point, I'd like to direct your attention to three special categories of trikes you might wish to explore further at your leisure. The first is the so-called "Fat" trike or "All-Terrain" trike, fitted with special tires and suspensions suitable for use on dirt trails. It's the trike equivalent of a mountain bike.

Fig. 8.15 Ice Full Fat in the snow

Fig. 8.16 Ice full Fat front

The second is the existence of "tandem trikes," two trikes linked together so that couples can enjoy the outdoors together, or alternatively, a physically impaired person can be towed along for an outdoor excursion. Delta trikes, like the Anura and Ketts, are especially well-suited to play these roles, but "tandems" are definitely available from tadpole manufacturers also.

Fig. 8.17 Hase Delta Trikes in Tandem

The third, in a category all by itself, is the **HP Velotechnik Scorpion Plus 20,** a tadpole trike whose seat height of up to 22.5 inches not only surpasses that of most others in its class but also that of most delta trikes.

Fig. 8.18 The HP Velotechnik Scorpion Plus 20

Designed specifically to meet the needs of the physically challenged, the Scorpion Plus 20, about four inches wider than normal trikes, is configured so that you can seat yourself without the inconvenience of straddling the main tube. And, as do most of its sister models, it accepts optional extras such as arm supports, crutch/cane holders. "stand-up aids," one hand controllers for the brakes and drivetrain, and special foot pedal arrangements that eliminate the need for clipless shoes. Its relatively high height places its riders much closer to the level of automobile drivers, while its full suspension makes for a comfortable ride. It folds easily, like its companion, the more normally configured Scorpion FX, which has a lower, but still accessible seat height of 14-19 inches.

Is a trike for you? Well, a recent online straw poll on the BentRider forum showed that almost 75 percent of the respondents had started triking after age 40 and some 50 percent after age 50. A look at photos of the most recent recumbent trade exhibition showed a preponderance of late middle-aged and senior visitors. One respondent to the poll said that because trikes were heavier and slower than regular bikes, there was no compelling reason to purchase one. Why, as this rider wrote, "trade a faster lighter ride for a seemingly slower heavy one?"

Not many trike owners would agree with him. In all of my reading about them in the last year, I've not once found a person who didn't love his or her trike. When all is said and done, thousands of bent riders look as eagerly forward to the cycling season as skiers do to the snow season. A recumbent trike is much more comfortable over a 30-mile ride than is a standard diamond bike, and they're almost as fast. For those of us who love tinkering with our toys, being a Bent owner offers myriad opportunities to add lights, pannier bags and bike computers along with lots of ways to fiddle with upgrading the drivetrain with derailleur systems and internal hubs of various speeds.

To my mind, with a recumbent bike, if you determine that you can mount it, get out of it, transport it and have a safe place to use it, then it's all gravy. And, when paired, as we will see next, with electric motors, they become even more useful and fun.

Chapter 9
There's a Lot to Like About E-Bikes

The bicycle world, in the years to come, will see the emergence of the e-assist bike and trike. In 2016, close to 250,000 e-bikes were sold in the United States. Yearly bicycle sales nationwide are 12.5 million.

Let's define exactly what these e-bikes are. In essence, they are electrically driven and—almost uniformly—lithium battery-supplied bikes. They operate either through small hub motors enclosed in the front or back wheel of a bike or through a mid-bike engine attached directly to the crankshaft. The latter, actually driving the chain, supplies direct motor power to the rear wheel.

These motors, by definition, are usually activated only by a rider's turning of the bike pedals. There are two ways that the motor knows that the pedals are turning: through the more common cadence sensor which directly counts the number of rotations of the pedals and adjusts speed accordingly, or the more expensive torque sensor, which correlates the amount of power sent to the unit to the physical effort exerted by the rider. The latter is more seamless and expensive. In both instances, the amount of overall power available is governed by the level set on your control panel: low, medium, or high; 1,2,3,4; or some other setting.

Electric motors provide riders with an assist, to help them either go faster or further than they could alone; to assist in powering the bike up a steep, otherwise difficult hill; or to help a tired biker glide easily home on that last four or five miles from an afternoon's excursion. E-bikes can either be pedaled by electricity alone or in conjunction with pedals, but in any case, by federal law, they must not be capable of going over 20 mph if powered by the engine alone. State laws are different and diffuse and may be more restrictive than those of the national government. More on that a bit later.

An e-bike, in its simplest form, Class 1, will not have a separate throttle. It may, however, have a start-assist mode wherein, if you push a dedicated button on the control panel, the motor will respond with an initial thrust of power to give you a running start before you begin to pedal. This is an important safety feature, particularly if you are stopped at a traffic light, or paused on an incline so steep that you can't even get started in first gear. Here you'll definitely need that boost. Class 2 bikes, in addition, are equipped with a separate throttle that can move the bike regardless of pedal movement. Class 3 bikes have no throttle, but pedal-assist motors that can reach up to 28 mph.

By law, these motors cannot be more than 750 watts, with most of them falling in the 250-watt measure. The range of the e-assist bike will vary, depending on the weight of rider and bike and the power of the engine, but almost all of them can go 20 miles on power alone.

Available now from such prestigious firms as Shimano, Bafang, Brose, and Bosch, they are great aids to those who are using their trikes as car substitutes, and if recreational, for those who wish to journey further afield. Consider that an adult trike can really only run between 5 and 10 mph, and see what a difference a motor can make.

What a sweet relief it is to know that, at the push of a button, you can have this marvelous electrical genie come out of the battery and give you a push along the way. In a sailboat analogy, it's like you've been beating into the wind and suddenly you reverse course, find the wind is behind you and are being pushed along by a gentle breeze. You don't lose your exercise benefits for you are still pedaling, but suddenly you find it's a lot easier, and you can go longer and further.

Had I last year, when I first started this search for an alternative to a car, been more knowledgeable about the constantly changing choices in low-step e-bikes, I might have made a different final choice. Following, after some research, are some two-wheel bikes that are worthy of consideration by a senior citizen who is somewhat physically impaired. All are under 20 inches in step-over height and well made.

They are the **Evolo Luna**, with a step-over height of 16½ inches, a 250-watt engine, a Nu Vinci 380 gear hub and a price below $2,000; the **Khalkhoff Agatu B7**, with an 18 inch step-over height, a Bosch mid-drive 250-watt engine, and a **Shimano Nexus 7** internal hub, and a price below $3000; the **Trek Lift Plus Lowstep**, which is 19.6 inches, with a Shimano ten speed derailleur and a mid-hub Shimano Steps 250 motor—about $2200; and the **SUN traditional trike** with a motor, a single speed with 24 inch wheels and a 15½ step through height.

There seems to be no standardization in nomenclature among bike manufacturers. Thus, "comfort," "low step," and "step-through" are used interchangeably, regardless of the actual distance of the lower tube from the ground.

Distinctly separate from the bikes above and in another class altogether would be the **Van Raam Balance bike**.

It has a step-through height of nine inches and its own well-developed range of 250-watt hub motors. This bike was actually designed to fit the needs of physically handicapped clientele, but it definitely is expensive, pricing out well above $4,000. A real competitor, priced lower, would be the **Pedego Boomerang**, available in a series of motor configurations, but also a true low-step with a nine-inch step-through height.

Fig. 9.1 Van Raam 'Balance' Bike

The 2017 Recumbent Cycle-Com tradeshow and convention was dominated by new electric trike offerings from the major manufacturers. Trident brought out an electric model based on its Spike, and TerraTrike, building on the frame of its popular Rambler model, has brought out the new **Evo**.

Fig. 9.2 Pedego Boomerang Plus

Both trikes, at $2,569 and $3,499, respectively, are well below the price of a similarly equipped, but fully suspended **Ice Adventure** model, which could run close to $8,000. But it has a deluxe system, which, according to its representative at the convention, almost replicates the action of an automatic transmission, seamlessly shifting between motor and gear combinations according to the felt needs of the triker. I've included the Adventure despite its seat height of 12.4 inches because you can add a "seat lifter" that will raise it up four inches, making it truly accessible to many more people, as is already the case with the Trident and TerraTrike models. Another fully suspended model is the **HP Velotechnik Scorpion 26 FS**. It can be purchased with a high seat

option that raises it to 15.33 inches. When decked out with its motor, it lists out at over $8,000.

A new engine, the **Copenhagen Wheel** self-described as "a sleek red hub that turns almost any bike into a smart electric hybrid," demonstrates the rapidly changing potential of e-assist bikes and trikes to revolutionize urban transportation in this country.

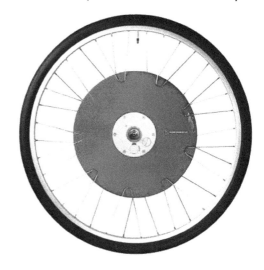

Fig. 9.3 Copehagen Wheel

Everything necessary to power your bike—motor, battery, sensors and control systems—is contained within that magical wheel that pairs itself seamlessly with your smartphone. This wheel can either replace the rear wheel of most bikes or be added to new bikes. The manufacturer declares: "Distances shorten, hills flatten and the experience becomes uniquely you, ride by ride." Using miniaturization, this new invention is inserted into a bike or trike's power wheel and immediately converts that vehicle into an e-assist model—no wires, no control, no throttle. It's like a robot that senses how fast you want to go, and then delivers a boost to your efforts. Developed by MIT engineers, and priced at just $1,500, controlled and paired with your iPhone and adaptable to diverse drivetrains, this is one solution for those who want to add power to their bikes. And there's a single-speed, step-through model, **the Kilt**, priced at $1,999.

Electric bikes are without doubt the wave of the future. Michigan is just the latest state to create a sensible legal structure to permit their use. But several obstacles—primarily environmentally and safety-based— remain to the widespread adoption of the electric bikes and trikes.

Amid the discussion leading up to legislation, a paper from Michigan's Environmental Council summed up the concerns: "Some trail advocates argue that many non-motorized trails should simply stay that way. There are also

very specific objections surrounding trail design and land access. The Michigan Mountain Biking Association, in a formally adopted policy, posits that long-fought-for access will be jeopardized, that e-bike riders may make the trail dangerous for other trail users, and that single track mountain bike trails that have been designed specifically and uniquely for non-motorized use could be damaged."

The council's paper, on the other hand, acknowledged the economic and social benefits of expanding e-bike use and greater public access to nature through them. The council cited favorably, as do many other actors in this debate, the case of California where Class 3 bikes can use bike lanes but are prohibited from bike trails, while Class 1 and 2 bikes can use them, except where prohibited by local law.

There's really a fear that electric bikes are like jet skis on a pristine lake, they will pollute the environment and destroy the solitude and peace that brings folks to bike trails in the first place. Then there are the bicycle purists—the no pain, no gain folks— who seem to think that if you're not pedaling, you're like Lance Armstrong.

"60 Minutes" did an exposé on this very subject. Well, let them be 70 years old with bum knees and stenosis, and see how much they would love to have an electric bike.

And then, there are those with even stronger objections, like New York City Mayor Bill de Blasio, who opened a short-lived vendetta against the throttle-driven e-bikes used extensively by restaurant take-out delivery riders. In 2017, the police confiscated 900 of them because the mayor said they're "too dangerous." By mid-2018, under intense pressure because his policy targeted low-paid immigrant laborers, the mayor relented and stated that legislation to make "Class I" e-bikes legal in the city was forthcoming. He also laid out plans to clarify the rules regulating throttle-driven electric bikes while his transportation chief, Polly Trottenberg, declared that "Cycling, including pedal-assist bikes is not only fun, it's a fast, affordable, healthy and sustainable way of getting around." New York City was finally falling in line with policies already in place in dozens of cities nationwide and around the world.

Countering what he considered to be the mayor's shortsightedness, a staff writer for *Slate*, Henry Grabar, reported: "A trial conducted by Portland State University researchers gave e-bikes to Kaiser Permanente employees, and found that after 10 weeks, the percent of participants who called themselves 'strong and fearless' or 'enthused and confident' bikers had risen from 38 to 52 percent. The number of people commuting once a week by bicycle more than doubled."

There's no doubt that the fear of e-bikes has been the overriding obstacle to their more widespread acceptance, and that, in turn, New York City's opposition has been key to maintaining their illegality in the state at large. But the Adirondacks and the Finger Lakes region could definitely find their tourist offerings enhanced by the possibility of attracting new electric bike users. With increased mobility, thousands of senior citizens could more broadly sample the wonderful offerings of nature in which these regions abound.

And the state's bicycle stores, now legally selling bikes that their new bike owners cannot legally use on the roads of New York, would be free to engage in the burgeoning e-bike market place. All over the country, new companies are arising with technological innovations in this field. New York needs to get on board and quickly.

The benefits of the e-bike are manifold. When used instead of cars, they reduce pollution and congestion. In the environmentally conscious Netherlands, e-bikes in 2016 made an astounding almost thirty percent of all bike sales."

E-bikes give folks, who have physical limitations and can no longer ride regular bikes, the ability to do so in style. They encourage bikers to roam more freely over longer distances; take away the fear of hills and fatigue and encourage people to exercise to their physical limit. The motor is always there to bring you home. The newest motors are silent indeed and not a noise pollutant. The psychological and physical benefits are legion. Just take a look at this comment from a thread concerning e-bikes:

"Navigated a 4,000-mile USA coast to coast this year with an electric assist. It was problem free and provided other benefits like evading dogs and unsafe road conditions. It also gave me higher miles per day. I'll never go back. At 74, I'm going to give it another big test in 2018."

In a small study of new e-bike riders at the University of Colorado, folks who'd never ridden them before indicated they were healthier with improved aerobic fitness and better blood sugar control. "They also reported finding the riding to 'be a blast,'" said William Byrnes, the study's senior author and director of the university's Applied Exercise Science Laboratory. "It's exercise that is fun." The report's startling conclusion was that "Pedelecs are an effective form of active transportation that can improve some cardio-metabolic risk factors within only four weeks."

From England, we have the testimony of one Phillip Dalton, who daily commuted back and forth to work on his electric bike: "The e-bike is brilliant as it helps me keep a good speed climbing up the hills, meaning that when I get to work, I'm not exhausted. It's almost as fast as taking the car, plus it's a great way to start the day. I love it. In the four months I've been using my e-bike, I've got much fitter without really noticing it and don't have to waste time at the gym because I've had my workout getting to the office."

Mr. Dalton has a California counterpart, Peter Compton, a seventy-nine-year-old, who on his birthday pedaled sixty miles round-trip to see his daughter. Said he, "My whole life, except for high school, I did no exercise—wore no spandex—until my doctor told me to last year," he said. "Now I love riding everywhere because it's so easy. I work up a sweat, but when there's a hill or a headwind, which would normally get me as white as a sheet from exhaustion, I cheat. I turn on the motor."

Some final thoughts and cautions on e-bikes. First of all, be careful when making your choice and weigh the possibility that your battery might run out and leave you in a position where you must pedal home. Left with only one speed and a 75-pound bike on your hands, you might be in a very rough spot because most trikes don't fold and AAA probably does not cover them for road service, although you should check with your local chapter as to the availability of such coverage.

Do you have a friend with a truck or van? If not, who's going to come get you? Will you have to leave your trike by the road? What's your physical condition and how's the weather out there in the boondocks? This is a strong reason for purchasing locally—the dealer might take pity on you—and making sure that your bike has multiple speeds. Indeed, in some cases, your local bike shop can order for you bikes that are advertised on the internet; you can have your cake and eat it too. A further good choice on your part might involve purchasing your bike primarily for its weight, gear range and general performance as a trike, and later add locally your choice of a well-known engine to be installed and serviced by your friendly bike mechanic.

Take care in your choice of an engine. In my case, when I had a slight problem with my motor, I really panicked. It turned out that the motor manufacturer was out of the e-bike business altogether. Fortunately, the maker of the trike stood strongly behind the product, and I received a phone call diagnosis that quickly solved my problem.

Besides the above listed cautions, sadly enough, there's a very serious and sobering statistic that a senior must consider before making a decision to purchase an electric bike. To wit, in the Netherlands in 2014, according to an article in Holland-Cycling.com, 107 out of the 185 cyclists killed in all cycle accidents were over age 65. The figure is not parsed out so as to indicate the number of those killed who were on electric bikes, but further statistics, cited in a *Guardian* article of September 22, 2017, sharpen that focus: In Holland, from 2014-16, 79 people were killed while on e-bikes "of whom 87 percent were over the age of 60."

The 74-year-old mother of Hillary Staples, the writer of the Holland-Cycling.com article, bought a new electric bike and shortly thereafter collided with a post and broke several bones. Staples alludes to the paradox caused by the ability of an e-bike to extend the riding life of seniors, while at the same time exposing them to new and unforeseen dangers. The same factors that begin to limit a senior's ability to drive a car—arthritis, diminished vision, slowed reflexes—are at play while attempting to drive an e-bike. In Holland, as a result, the police are asking for laws to require safety courses before individuals are certified to ride e-assist bikes. And others have suggested that seniors take a voluntary test to ferret out and correct any difficulties they might have in adjusting to the new riding experience offered by an e-assist bike.

In my opinion, any senior contemplating the purchase of an e-bike should definitely get an okay from their physician before embarking on this great new adventure. The doctor knows best, and it's better to be safe than sorry.

The above concerns aside, I've really enjoyed my e-bike experience. It's been a ray of sunshine in my daily life. I think I'll know—as was the case with cars—when to throw in the towel and call it quits. And that will be one sad day, believe me!

Chapter 10
I Make My Choice—An Adult Comfort Electric Trike

The trike lover who brought the low-lying one over to my house for a trial strongly suggested that I'd be better off with a three-wheel adult trike, "You know, the ones that you see the old folks using." Then, after a glance around the complex where I live, he said, "Why, you've got enough room here to make a circuit without going out on the road."

Well, after trying the recumbent trikes, with their accessibility and unloading problems, I'd pretty well decided that I should take another look at an adult trike.

The adult trike in its most basic form is nothing more or less than a replica of the tricycles lots of us had when we were kids. They'd been in the periphery of my sight, but I'd not really been interested in them because they looked a bit stodgy. You sat high up in them, and, on the web, some bent

riders labeled them "tippy" and "unstable" compared to their low-slung machines.

They were at least worth a look, so earlier, Fred and I had hopped in his car and headed out to a suburb just after a snowstorm to look at a trike. It was a beautiful, yellow machine, made to be a cargo vehicle in factories. This one had been used mainly by an electronic salesman to navigate his way around trade shows. Its step-through height, at 15 3/8 inches, was relatively low. Here, we had the obverse problem from that of the recumbent trike: If your body's hurting, you want a low step-over height, something around 15 inches or below, instead of a higher height that's important for a recumbent trike.

I engaged the parking brake and was just barely able to get my stenosis-affected leg over the crossbar so I could take a position on the trike. It took a bit of time to adjust to this one, particularly to its tendency to pull to one side. The situation seems common with most lower- or medium-priced trikes without differentials, although folks do adjust to it. I was also put off by its high height. I really felt far from the ground.

So, I passed on this trike, which not only had a parking brake, but also a three-speed shifter, a necessity for an adult trike unless you're always going to be on level ground. Indeed, it's critical because the leg strength of older people is just not there. Nevertheless, you'll find that some of the most popular adult trikes only come in single-speed versions, a good reason to reject them if you think you'll be encountering any kind of a hill or incline

After some more thought and reading, I figured I'd give them another chance. This time I approached it more methodically as recommended by adult-trike manufacturers. Let me summarize. For starters, it's important that the new rider have someone stabilize the trike by holding the handlebars while the rider acclimates himself to its unfamiliar ways. To wit, it's not the same as with a two wheel-bike, when your body moves with the

bike and determines its direction. Try this with a trike, and you might suddenly find yourself on the ground.

Instead, the front wheel steers the trike, just like a tiller on a boat. Your body needs to sit firmly upright, knees well inboard and eyes looking forward, not down at the ground. This is not a natural feeling for longtime bicycle riders, which is one reason why some trike manufacturers say those who've never ridden a bike are sometimes more at ease on a trike.

With the aid of that helper, you'll slowly gain your confidence. Once you've done so, you can go out to a parking lot or schoolyard on a Sunday and start doing figure eights until you're comfortable with the trike.

Then, and only then, should you try to turn into a driveway. Two or three of my younger neighbors did it and almost turned my trike over by leaning too sharply. Adult trikes can be ornery creatures if not attended to properly. "I assumed, wrongly, that three wheels would be safer," writes Susan Watkins on the "Tricycle for Adults" blog, ". . . but after swerving onto a grass verge and then back onto the canal path near my home and going dizzy trying to balance on surfaces with a camber, I now know better!" And you definitely don't want to be in a situation where you're trying to ride across a street and find that you don't have the leg strength to beat the oncoming traffic.

Now, how do you go about selecting a suitable adult trike? You'll find that most bike stores don't stock them since they take up too much floor space and appeal to a limited audience. So after looking at some factors that should affect your choice, I'll point to some trikes that are worth your considered attention.

But as you peruse the online reviews of the lower-priced bikes, you'll find complaint after complaint about missing bolts and screws, fenders that don't fit and rattle, wheels that are out of true, seats that slip down into the tube, missing pedals, chains that fall off and inoperative brakes. Most of the trikes under $400 come out of China, although some come from Taiwan. Many of them seem to be just boxes of cut metal, with minimal instructions therein about how to assemble them.

Be prepared to have your new trike assembled by your local bike shop, and that, depending on the complexity of the job is going to cost $75-150. Plus, factor in getting the boxed trike to and from the bike shop. Most of them don't fold and therefore won't fit in the trunk of your car for easy transportation.

On the other hand, you can opt to assemble your new trike yourself. But, if you really want to give yourself some smiles on a bad day, just set about reading some online reviews about this process—they're full of complaints from folks who spent whole days putting them together, sometimes to get close to the end only to find that a cable or pedal was missing. It's not for the faint of heart. Even some former bike mechanics have trouble putting them together. Thankfully, Amazon and some other retailers will ship your new trike directly to a shop of your choice to solve this problem

The next thing you need definitely to check is the step-through height. I can't emphasize this too much, for 15 inches is barely tolerable if you have neuropathy, stenosis or hip or knee problems. If you have lots of trouble getting up from a chair or are anywhere near using a lift chair, lower is better. Just because a trike has "step-through" in its description doesn't mean it's suitable for you.

Check the shifting system on the trike. Is it single-speed, three-speed, or seven- or eight-speed? The more speeds, the better. It's rare that you can find any of these trikes with the 24-speed derailleur that is almost standard on road bikes, although, with proper modification, it can be done.

Again, as pointed out earlier, if the trike is seven- or eight-speed, is it a regular derailleur system, the one with seven or eight cogs in the back and a shifter on the handlebar, or is it an internal hub, just a smooth bulb in the back? If it's the latter and your trike is at a standstill, you'll be able to shift down to a low gear to start again. If the former, then you might find yourself in the impossible situation of having to start from a high gear if you forgot to shift down before coming to a stop.

Next, check the seat for comfort and adjustment. Does it have a quick adjust feature, or does it require a wrench or screwdriver to move it up or down? How comfortable is the seat? Leather or plastic? Remember now that you are using the trike for comfort, not for speed. Try it out if you can. Would

you be comfortable sitting in it for hours on end?

How about the brakes? Does it have front "direct pull" brakes, commonly called under their Shimano trademarked name as "V-brakes" and back step-on brakes? Or does it have disc brakes? Does it have a parking brake? Are there reflective features on the back and on the sidewalls of the tires?

Does it have fenders? If so, are they integrally built into the body of the trike? If they're separate, they may bang and chatter a lot. And, by the way, is there a chain guard to stop your pants legs from being caught in the chain? Check out the pedals for sturdiness of construction and anti-slip features. What you're after is a smoothly operating machine that's not going to mess up your wonderful springtime ride.

Check too on the tire size. Twenty inches is decent, 24 is better, and 26-inch wheels just might be too large for an elderly citizen to handle.

Does it have a basket? Plastic or metal?

Having said all that, besides the ever-popular Schwinn trikes, Sun trikes, like the one I almost bought, are good. And you might want to add the **Worksman trike**, another established manufacturer. In this same category might be the new **Raleigh Tri-Star** with a step-through height of 13¾ inches.

Also in the ballgame is the well-constructed **Mission Solo** with a step-through height of six inches. British-designed and assembled, it comes with a large basket, sealed wheel bearings, a padded seat, six-speed Shimano hub system, 20-inch wheels and a parking brake. At this point, you're well into the $800 range for your trike, but look at the low step-over height!

Fig. 10.1 Mission Solo

Another quality trike, but somewhat cheaper, is the **Belize Tri-Rider Capri** with a step-over height of 14 inches. Equipped with a six-speed Shimano derailleur, it's just below $500. All of the above are traditional-

looking upright trikes that will serve you well.

There is another category of upright trikes called semi-recumbents, bridging the gap between the uprights and the fully recumbent trikes we've earlier examined. Semi-recumbent trikes are defined by upright handle bars, reclined seats, sometimes with a backrest, comfortable saddles and crankshafts that are 10-12 inches forward of the usual position. You'd be lucky indeed to find one of these trikes priced south of $1,000.

But there is a real bargain in this category: **the Belize Tri-Rider R-2**, a mixed version of a Delta trike in that it has handle bars up front rather than a crankshaft. Like a Delta, it has a large sling seat in place of the usual adult trike saddle. Beautifully designed, it has a 21-speed derailleur system, and that's plenty of gear inches to deal with most hills. It has 20-inch wheels, a really comfortable seat height of 21 inches and a step-over height of 18 inches. With a weight limit of 300 pounds, it's also supplied with rear disc brakes and the familiar front V-brake. Unfortunately, it does not have a differential, and when you do go to purchase a semi-recumbent trike with one, you're talking serious money indeed.

A standout in this category is the **Van Raam Easy Rider**, which in 2017 was certified by an Independent Government Commission in Norway as the "Best Product" in the semi-recumbent bike category. It's not cheap, coming in around $3,000, single speed, and a good $3,500 with an eight-speed device. It has a very low center of gravity, so it is easily mounted. The step-through height is six inches, and a superbly streamlined design incorporates such aspects as a built-in security lock. This, along with the similarly featured and expensive PFIFF scooter-trike, would obviously be my first choice for easy mounting and comfort in an adult trike.

Fig. 10.3 Van Raam Easy Rider with Motor

Fig. 10.4 PFIFF Scooter Trike

What do these costly vehicles have in common? First of all, they have differentials to drive the rear wheels. This greatly enhances the handling of the trikes on hills, on cambered roads and in making turns of all sorts. These trikes are impressively engineered, every part hand-assembled by German or Dutch mechanics. And they probably drive, if my PFIFF is an example, wonderfully well—just like a Mercedes. Are they worth $2,000 more than an adult trike made in China? That's debatable indeed, but in the case of

Fig. 10.2 Easy Rider

the Van Raam Easy Rider, the dealer says he can't keep them in stock.

Fig. 10.5 A Row of Van Raam Special Needs Trikes

A much less costly option would be the **Belize semi-recumbent Comfort Tri-Rider**, which costs $700 with a step-over height of 14½ inches. It's a stretched-out version of the Capri 24, with a backrest. Sitting slightly higher than the Van Raam or PFIFF scooter trike, it's really a bargain, semi-recumbent trike with many characteristics of the best European trikes. But again, it has no differential. It should also be noted that Belize has a folding trike, altogether worthy of your attention.

To sum things up, I'd like to turn to turn to my own search for a semi-recumbent trike. After my experience with the first trike, I was determined to find one with a differential. And I

determined that this particular feature almost invariably went along with better construction, stronger and lighter metals, better paint jobs, expert welding, and—upon delivery—almost fully assembled trikes.

And so we come to the **PFIFF Comfort Electric Ansmann**. By the spring of 2017, I'd come to some kind of a decision. I knew I wanted a very low step-through height on whatever vehicle I selected. And I was pretty sure I wanted a semi-recumbent comfort trike. I still don't totally understand the niche into which comfort trikes fit in the semi-recumbent category, but I think that their primary traits are a very low step-through height, a plush seat and long, upright handlebars.

Fig. 10.6 PFIFF Comfort Trike

My choice finally settled on the PFIFF brand which had a series of comfort trikes. I wanted a quality trike because I'd been spooked by the litany of complaints about the poor quality and myriad problems experienced by the owners of the cheaper models of trikes. And, at my age, I didn't want to assemble a trike. By luck one night, I was browsing for PFIFF trikes and suddenly saw for sale on eBay their comfort trike with an electric assist motor. It was "open box." I bid for it, and five days later a big package arrived by UPS. The package was so distressed that I hesitated to accept it. In the course of three minutes, I changed my mind three times. Finally, the driver opened the box up for me to see:

"Hey, mister, look at it, not a scratch on it." He shook his head. "It's a real beauty. Looks like it would be fun."

He was right. One look at this machine and I was sold. But I definitely didn't like the fact that it had cost me $2,300, even though its list price was $3,200, and I knew it was a bargain. After all, I'd never paid more than $500 for a bike in my life.

"I'll take it. Where do I sign?"

I put it into the garage, discarded the huge box and looked at this mechanical miracle in front of me. Every part of it spelled quality. The body was powder-coated, every connection TIG-welded. In this process, an electrified tungsten rod is enclosed in a tube with shielding argon gas. When turned on, the instrument forms an electronic arc with the target metal, thus, melting it. "Gas tungsten arc welding" gives the mechanic very precise control over the time and temperature of the weld, resulting in smooth and strong joints. PFIFF is a long-standing German company whose alphabetical title disguises the fact that it focuses on one thing—giving mobility to disabled people and, in the process, giving their lives back to them. It has an imposing list of trikes of all sorts, marked most significantly by their accessibility.

Within an hour, I was ready to roll. What kind of a trike was it? First of all, its step-over height was only 10 inches, and that definitely marked it off from practically all of the Chinese and Taiwanese competitors. It takes precision engineering and skilled welding to make the components of a quality step-over trike because it's devoid of the strength given by the dual-tube setup of most bikes.

The trike was delivered already assembled—the only thing I had to do was to drop the seat into its tube. And what a seat it was, wide, fully cushioned and made of expensive and supple leather. It was a seat that you could ride on—as I was to experience later—for hours on end without feeling any pain whatsoever. Read over the reviews for cheaper trikes, and you'll find that uniformly the buyers complain about seat discomfort, frequently solving the problem by discarding the original seat and buying something more suitable.

Moreover, the comfort seat was quickly and infinitely adjustable, with the click of a strong and bulletproof lever. There was no slippage. The handlebars, too, were almost infinitely adjustable, making the trike usable for both young and old in a family, should, as was not my case, the elder wish to share the trike with others.

The trike, let's call it Suzy Mae, was very easy to mount. You could literally ease yourself back into the seat (it had a back support) without lifting your feet over the lower tube. Once firmly seated, you could then lift a leg right over the tube with no trouble at all.

Suzy Mae was most of all, accessible. The whole setup of the trike made you want to use it.

Its next most important feature was the differential for the two back wheels that made them turn in synchronized fashion. It was, in effect, two-wheel drive, and that distinguished this adult trike from just about every other one out there, except those made by Van Raam. It was a very stable trike, characterized also by front "v" brakes and rear coaster brakes.

Its regular drive train was a seven-speed Shimano internal hub, controlled by a grip on the right front handle. It shifted smoothly, could be changed while at rest, and most importantly, shifted down to first gear when waiting to cross a street.

I can't emphasize how important it is that you decide what you want in a trike. If your aim is both exercise and mobility for trips to the library and local shopping, then you must be sure that your trike has at least seven speeds.

Finally, my Suzy Mae came with front and rear fenders that were permanently attached to the body of the trike. It also had an adjustable backrest with a lumber support.

As an adjunct to all of the above attributes, the trike was delivered with a real bonus to me, an e-assist motor. I had initially not shopped for a trike with a motor, but I was very satisfied when I saw that this "bargain" trike came with one.

Now, I'm sure the reader wants to know exactly what my experience on the trike was. First of all, I watched several times a series of how-to-ride-a-trike videos put out by PFIFF—you can find them on YouTube. Then I gingerly set forth around the quad, slowly at first. Then—86 years old and 215 pounds—I began to drive around easily, shifting with speed and accuracy between the different gradations on the shifter. It was smooth as could be. The seven speeds definitely seemed adequate for most of the rather moderate terrain around my neighborhood, but I had to use second, and sometimes even first gear to move up my rather steep driveway.

Later, I really ventured afield, and sometimes, when close to cresting a hill, almost felt that I had to use my motor, which I did. I really don't know how to compare my fitness with that of others, but simply say I'm glad I have the motor to kick in when necessary.

As to the comfort of this trike, it's truly amazing. It rides smoothly and confidently, with nary a squeak or a rattle—walking neighbors call it the "silent machine." It's really a cruising trike, and a good day of sunshine and blue skies up here in the Albany area quickly transmutes in my mind to a good day on our beautiful Lake George, 100 miles to the north.

Once I'm on this trike, everything is good with my soul. In five months, I've put 1,000 miles on it, riding twice a day most days. Have I taken it on trails? No, because transporting it has definitely been an issue since it doesn't fold, I don't drive anymore, and I have little access to friends with trucks.

There were well-reviewed folding adult trikes available (the Italian-made **DeBlasi-r32** is one), but some seemed to be of questionable solidity, step-over height was too high, or their frames were too small for a full-sized adult like me. I have ventured far and wide in my neighborhood, but with the advice of seasoned neighbors around here basically stayed off of heavily trafficked roads. Partially, I've been constrained by the New York law concerning e-assist bikes and by friends who think that, despite signs and things, I'll be run over by some fool or another out there.

I still have not used the motor very much but do run it every few days just to keep it in tune. You're not going to break speed records with a Suzy Mae, but if you're like me, hurting a bit physically and well into old age, you're not out to set any new road records anymore. You just want to enjoy the freedom and memories of mobility that a solidly built trike like this can bring to you as you cruise around the neighborhood and stop by the stores to pick up the morning paper and have a cup of coffee. The neighbors are still awed by the excellent construction of this vehicle. One noted how the fenders are actually attached to its frame so as to assure they are rattle-free.

My comfort trike came with a bell that was definitely loud enough indeed to meet the state regulations that it be heard within 100 feet radius of the bike. On my morning and evening rides around the complex, I used to ring it whenever I saw a youngster. They would turn and wave. One day, in the midst of deep thought on some seemingly serious matter, I failed to ring it as I passed a three-year-old. His father took him on a walk every evening. Realizing my mistake, I looked back over my shoulder. The young boy stood waving after me and my bike. Feeling bad, I turned around, and, for the first time, let the youngster, lifted up by his Dad, ring the bell himself.

From then on, that was part of the evening ritual. He just had to ring the bell, or neither of our days would be complete. And too, if truth be told, I liked to hear the ringing of the bell myself—it reminded me of the Italian water ice man who would come through the neighborhood when I was a kid in Philly. He pushed a cart that contained a block of ice and bottles full of the most delicious juices—orange, strawberry, lemon and vanilla. He'd ring that bell—"ding-dong," and we kids would come running fast as we could, pennies in our pockets, to buy our water ices. I think I had a bit of that feeling every time I rang my little bell.

Of course, I had to equip my bike with a computer. For who can have a good exercise routine without some way of measuring speed, time and distance of a workout. There were literally dozens of choices in this regard, but as a longtime user of Garmin nautical instruments, I quickly narrowed my choice down to its bike computers line.

And there I had to pick from a confusing mix of choices. Garmin's cheapest models were the **Edge 20** and **Edge 25**, both small watch-sized devices capable of displaying in clear digits average speed, distance and elapsed time. Both models have rudimentary mapping capabilities—you can trace your route or download a prearranged route from your computer. Both models are capable of linking with **Garmin Express**, an app that displays and stores your exercise results. They can also link up with the worldwide **Strada exercise network** where you can share your results with others and engage in bike-related social activities. The devices can be set with distance-related sound alerts and are equipped with auto-pause functions, so you won't become impatient when you stop to pass the time of day with a neighbor. The exercise tracker stops automatically when it senses a lack of

forward motion on your part and starts when you start cycling again.

The primary difference between the Garmin 20 and 25 is the latter's Bluetooth capability that lets you download your day's workout data to your phone or computer without a cable. Also, if you have your phone with you, text and phone notifications can be displayed while you're riding. The 25, moreover, has a feature, through **Garmin Connect** whereby your friends and family can track your progress during your journey. Finally, the 25 can hook up to heart-rate sensors and speed and cadence sensors whose results you can download to your phone. As an added bonus, heart rate measurements can be found on the display itself.

Yes, there are significant differences between the two models, but if you're like me and just want a good measuring stick to track daily activities, then the Edge 20 is fine—and a lot cheaper than the 25.

Both models are small but highly visible while cycling even to my senior eyes. They are easily mounted and dismounted by a twist of the wrist on the provided holder. I usually leave my

20 to charge overnight on my computer—you can't plug it into a wall outlet—and once charged, for me, it has a life of six or seven hours. It's possible to spend double or triple the cost of an Edge 25 for a Garmin bike computer—the popular Edge 520, comes to mind—and with these devices come larger screens, color, longer battery life and actual maps just as on a regular GPS. But I found the Edge 20 to be sufficient for my needs as I didn't foresee any long-distance touring or racing in my immediate future!

Why use any computer, you might ask, when you can simply use the GPS on your phone? The simple answer is that GPS use rapidly depletes a cell phone's battery, and you just might need to use that phone for emergency calls. Better to keep it charged and use a Garmin or its equivalent.

There remained the matter of equipping my trike with a set of lights. Again, this was a confusing and time-consuming exercise, but it was definitely necessary in my situation to have both front and rear lights. I settled on a front light from **Exposure**, a British manufacturer of high quality portable lights, primarily because of the long life of the self-contained battery. No unwieldy wires or cables here. Charged overnight, it will run for close to an hour on a high beam and literally for five to six hours on lower exposure levels. These are easily changed by pushing a handy control button at the business end of the light.

Its beam was wide enough and bright enough to have my neighbors remark on how "safe that must make you feel when it's getting dark around here." Cars immediately slowed when they saw me coming and I, in turn, with a slight twist of the wrist, would deflect the lamp downward so as to avoid blinding them with its powerful beam.

A red-textured glow ring at the tip enhanced its effect in the emergency flashing mode. About five inches in length, sturdy but light in weight, my **Exposure Axiom lamp** could also be used as a helmet light. As a bonus, it came with a lanyard so it could become an ordinary flashlight when off the bike. Although the Axiom is now discontinued, a similar model, the **Exposure Switch**, is one of the more popular lamps.

For the rear light, I chose the well-known **Light and Motion Vis 180**. It definitely is visible from the sides and rear and has a long battery life— enough for at least a week's worth of one-hour twilight rides.

Well, I could go on and on, but let me summarize my experience with the Pfiff comfort trike by saying that, though expensive, it is worth the price. I'm thankful every day that I get on it and head out for my morning ride. And, as equipped now, it's all set to roll safely as dusk approaches. Hope this helps as you move into your search for the perfect substitute steed for that car! Keep on moving!

Chapter 11
Wrapping Up the Journey

As we wrap up our journey through the continually changing world of personal mobility devices, let's try to place biking for seniors in the broader context of the worldwide cycling revolution. Within the last four years, an organization called **Cycling without Age** has enjoyed rapid international growth. It was founded by Ole Kassow, a Dane who wanted to find a way of helping disabled and immobile seniors to once again enjoy the outdoors and "feel the wind in their hair." Thought led to action, and Kassow, together with Dorthe Pedersen, a friend and community consultant, designed five trishaws—modified cargo trikes—with seats for two seniors in front. They could then be transported for a ride out into the fresh air.

Cycling Without Age is founded on the principles of bringing joy to old folks by the simple act of restoring to them a sense of mobility, creating and renewing a bond between old and young, cycling "slowly" so that riders and passengers can better enjoy the sights of nature, and encouraging folks of all ages to listen and learn from each other's tales and stories—bridging the generation gap and creating a higher sense of community and togetherness. As of today, there are over 1,000 chapters worldwide, with a good 10,000 volunteer "pilots" trained to bike the elderly safely around on these trikes. The pilots come from all walks of life with the only qualification being a willingness to serve and ability to cycle.

Fig. 11.1 An Outing

The primary vehicle used is a trishaw called the **Triobike Taxi**, a strongly constructed and plushly equipped pedestrian taxi with a vehicle-stowable outdoor plexiglass cover and a special removable middle plate on the footrest that permits easy entry. Each taxi comes complete with a blanket and a storage compartment beneath the seats for a picnic box or snacks. Many of the 117-pound trikes are equipped with e-assist motors to help the pilots and the standard 9-speed Shimano Deore internal hub to deal with hills.

At a cost of over $5,000 and close to $10,000 fully equipped with a motor, the Triobike seems to have been primarily purchased by senior facilities, religious organizations and impromptu locally organized groups that have banded together and formed chapters of Cycling Without Age. In the U.S. there are already chapters in at least 20 states. The combination of exercise, charity and fellowship has been a strong stimulus to the organization's spread. What can be better than to have cycled five miles, burned off 200 calories, enjoyed good conversation and brought a sparkle to the eyes of an elderly soul in need of a healing touch.

Ole Kassow's brainchild is but one manifestation of the global surge in the use of bicycles. **The Bicycling and Walking in the United States 2014 Benchmarking Report** lays out the many ways in which bikes—despite New York City's retrograde assault on electric bikes—are the wave of the future in urban transportation. Transportation overloads, automobile pollution and congestion are making life difficult for city dwellers and commuters alike.

One result is that urban planners have increasingly tried to make cities bike-friendly in the course of adopting what are called the "complete streets" planning platform. The concept demands that streets be planned and reconfigured to be accessible to pedestrians, bikers, the disabled and automobiles alike. That's a tall order indeed, but planners have come up with some well-developed strategies, particularly for cycling.

Thus, we increasingly find walled-off and uniquely colored bike lanes, and "bike box" intersections where the stop line for bikes is positioned far ahead of that line for automobiles, making it easier for bikers to make a left turn at a stop light. It also gives the biker a head start in moving through the intersection and decreases the likelihood that a car turning right will clip a cyclist coming up from behind.

Some of the more advanced cities have set up special bike racks close to the means of mass transportation, easing the safe transition of riders from their bikes to the train or bus. Indeed, the idea has even been broached of establishing bike buses as a way of collecting bikers at a central point outside the metropolitan area and transporting both passengers and their bikes to the center of the city where they could pedal to their final destinations.

Even more creative has been a movement to use urban bike trails, often overlaid on former railroad tracks, as safe and viable alternate means for cyclists to commute into the heart of cities. Secure bike racks, weather shelters, and shuttle buses would await them to complete the journey to their offices. Such innovations might stimulate the growth of small businesses at both ends of the trail.

Bike trails in rural areas, while mainly used by walkers and bikers, have increased commerce at stops along the way. I commend to you in this regard the beautiful 14-mile-long Kokosing Gap trail in central Ohio that winds through the verdant countryside connecting the towns of Mount Vernon, Gambier, Howard, and Danville. Planted on the base of a former railroad line, one showpiece is a restored 1940 Alco 0-6-0 locomotive with a red caboose that stands beside the trail close to the campus of Kenyon College. Indeed, it was at that very spot, some 70 years ago that, suitcase in hand, I clambered down the steel stairs of a coach to begin my sophomore year at Kenyon. I walked parts of this path a few years back with my Dolomite Jazz Walker.

It's an exciting time to be alive as a biker, young or old. Cities across the country have created bike-share programs, both dockless and docked, in places as diverse and different as Washington, Los Angeles, and San Francisco. In January 2018, Uber joined with the e-bike vendor and renter,

JUMP, to facilitate the dockless rental of electric bikes in San Francisco for a new program called Uber Bike. Shortly thereafter, in April 2018, Uber purchased JUMP as a prelude to expanding the Uber Bike initiative nationwide. JUMP had already launched a program with the city of Providence, Rhode Island that will put 400 electric dockless bikes on its streets in the summer of 2018. Just sign up online, obtain a PIN number, unlock an available electric bike with it, ride to your destination, leave the bike in any bike rack or locked to an available light post, and go about your merry way.

The increased use of bikes as alternatives to cars and the movement to facilitate this trend are mutually reinforcing: the easier and safer it is to commute by bike, the more people will be encouraged to do so. The benefits to cities and riders are manifest for both, but particularly so for the health of the cyclists.

According to a 2012-2014 survey cited by the National Institutes of Health, 2 out of 3 adult Americans are overweight or obese. It's well established by now that these conditions are associated with such problems as high blood pressure, diabetes and arthritis. Yet a major study published in the British Medical Journal in 2017 that examined the commuting habits of over 263,450 subjects during a five-year period in Wales, Scotland and Great Britain came to the astonishing conclusion, as summarized by *Forbes* magazine on April 25, 2017, that: "Commuters who cycled to work had a 41 percent lower risk of dying from all causes than people who drove or took public transport. They also had a 46 percent lower risk of developing and a 52 percent lower risk of dying from cardiovascular disease, and a 45 percent lower risk of developing and a 40 percent lower risk of dying from cancer." Done by a team of researchers at the University of Glasgow, this survey is perhaps the strongest piece of empirical data yet to undergird the push for the expansion of bike friendly infrastructure in all possible phases of American life. And that study's conclusion is undergirded by yet another research finding, reported by *The New York Times* on March 14, 2018, that "doing lots of exercise in older age can prevent the immune system from declining and protect people against infections." Indeed, that experiment, based on a study group of 125 long distance cyclists, some in their eighties, found that the seniors had "the immune systems of 20-year-olds."

Recent developments point toward a bike-centric future, hopefully with row after row of gleaming bikes and trikes neatly parked along the sidewalks of communities across the country.

It will be a major and much-needed step forward in the ongoing struggle to preserve the planet and its people from the ravages of air pollution and climate change. At the same time, it will knit communities closer together and encourage citizens young and old to engage in healthy outdoor activities that bring about bountiful benefits to their physical and mental well-being.

Epilogue

As you see, the motivating factor for the creation of this book was my own loss of the physical ability to drive a car. But there were other factors indeed: retirement after 55 years of teaching and my forced step-down from my church's male chorus. Yes, after 30 years there, somebody, understandably, decided that my inability to make the Thursday night rehearsals was grounds for retirement.

One Sunday morning a year or so ago, without forewarning, the pastor called my name and asked would I please step forward. He then nodded to the choir's president who, standing by the pastor, suddenly took a plaque out from behind his back and presented it to me. Inscribed on it was my designation as "Member Emeritus" of the Male Chorus and thanks for my many years of service! What could I do, but smile and graciously accept it? I was done and would sing no more. And I loved to sing, even made a CD of hymns many years ago.

Further, as is the case when growing old, I had lost a lot of friends. When I came to Albany 30 years ago, I made several good friends. One was Deacon Ernest Williams, a World War II D-Day veteran and the strong anchor of my church. He was the head chef of the church's soup kitchen and made a delicious chicken gumbo that was the delight of the Saturday afternoon visitors who came to partake of it. Solomon-like, he was someone you could turn to for advice, knowing that he'd not steer you wrong.

Another good friend was Carson Carr, a giant of a man, a native Philadelphian like myself, and a famed administrator of the Educational Opportunity Program at the university where I taught. We loved to spend time talking about the old days in the City of Brotherly Love, even though I'd left town for college when he was still in elementary school. He was a vital connection to my youth—just the mention of a name of a street or a famous high school athlete, or the Eagles, could launch us into an hours-long discussion.

Every Thursday, the three of us would frequent a Chinese restaurant that had a succulent buffet for all of $5.

There we'd sit, talk and discuss the events of the day and, sometimes, life's sorrows and joys. We were just plain buddies, and I missed them when they passed on—the Deacon in 2013, Carson in 2014. These losses were followed by the death of my younger brother, Forrest Ballard, a retired policeman and Korean War Marine vet, in 2015. And just last year, my best friend from college and football teammate, Stanley L. Jackson, passed away.

What's all of this have to do with a book on trikes? Well, they're definitely mixed together. As you age, friends and kin are going to pass away, and you'll be increasingly isolated, as one by one those who were dear to you depart.

In my own case, the cumulative impact was that I felt very alone. I'd even stopped going to the Y where I'd been a faithful and active member for a good 20 years. I'd done that because a re-do of the locker room had markedly decreased the available space and it had become very difficult with my various ailments to shower and dress without bumping into people.

In short, when I began this journey into the world of mobile devices, I was under a lot of stress, and the search itself became a means of relieving those pressures. For months at a time—too distracted to focus on academic matters—I'd plunge myself into the world of trikes or bicycles, surfing the web, examining and imbibing minute data on seat heights or crankshaft measurements as if they were the most important things in the world

And indeed, they were because they distracted me from the life-changing events impinging on my psyche. Through the fall and the winter, the search for a car substitute engrossed me as once did, earlier in life, my search for a new car, except now I had a new enabler—the internet— open and inviting me to while away hours searching for that best rollator or adult trike. It was a form of therapy, as much so as were my early morning walks that I continued on my rollator through the winter, except in the most severe weather. It took a blizzard to make me stay home.

Finally, I found peace in the music of the church. Particularly in the hymns that have lasted over time and speak of the triumph of love over tragedy, of peace amidst storms. This was the music that I heard in my youth and to which I now return in my twilight years. And, strangely enough, that's all the music that I wish to hear now. YouTube has become my default radio station. Here I can listen to calming gospel-infused versions of hymns like "Leaning on the Everlasting Arms," "It is Well with My Soul" and "Jesus, Lover of My Soul."

Ah, and now what about the trike? Well, after I put it into operation, my life changed. It arrived in mid-May, and by the end of the month, I was routinely biking an hour in the morning and an hour in the evening. And it was during those times that my mind would run free. I'd enjoyed many a good hour in my little sailboat on Lake George, and now, that I couldn't sail anymore, I had a wonderful substitute—Suzy Mae.

Gliding along, I'd sometimes imagine myself back aboard my little craft. It was good for mind and body. It was while on the trike that the idea came to me to write this little book to serve as a beginning guide to those who wanted to remain mobile and to use technological advances to help them to that end.

You'll find far more detail as you begin your own searches, but hopefully, I will have given you a head start and helped to narrow down the selection process. As to my own final selection of an adult trike over a recumbent trike, let me just say that I'm very satisfied with my choice. I feel safer in it as it puts my head on the same level as that of a driver of a car—my eyes and those of the driver meet.

And it's truly accessible in that you just hop on your trike as you did when you were a kid and ride off. There's no need as with a recumbent trike to have special shoes, or for biking clothing. And frankly, given the traffic patterns in my townhouse complex with a few roundabouts that tend to conceal oncoming cars, I'd feel unsafe driving a recumbent trike. But I do, sometimes, hanker for a bit more speed and excitement in my daily rides, and there are some beautiful bike paths along the Mohawk and Hudson rivers. Hmm? Could one of those shiny, fast-moving, suspended, recumbent folding trikes end up as a stablemate to Suzy Mae one day? Who knows? Stranger things have happened in my life.

Well, this ends our journey. And I can do no better here than to quote the words of Albert Einstein, "Life is like riding a bicycle. To keep your balance, you must keep moving."

See you down the road!

Bibliography

Below I have listed other resources, both print and digital, to aid the reader in further research on some of the topics covered in the text. My choices of these sources are selective, and they include some useful material furnished by interested parties such as manufacturers and commercial outlets. I should point out, in passing, that some so-called "books," particularly on topics such as electric bikes, are nothing more than barely concealed and hastily thrown-together advertisements for a particular brand. But, in general, you should have lots of good reading ahead of you!

Ball, Bryan. *How Recumbents Are Exactly Like Beer*, Kindle edition. BentRider Books, 2013. A compilation of articles written by the dean of recumbent bikes and present managing editor of the major recumbent website, Bentrider Online. Excellent material on the history of recumbent bikes in the United States.

Bernstein, David; *Senior Driving Dilemmas: Lifesaving Strategies,* Kindle edition. Dynamic Learning, 2015. An introduction to the topic by a geriatric physician.

De Boer, Frank; *The Rollator, My Best Friend*. American Star Books, 2015. A short, but very helpful and detailed guide to the use of rollators by a longtime leader of rollator clinics in the Netherlands.

Dugan, Elizabeth. *The Driving Dilemma: The Complete Resource Guide for Older Drivers and Their Families*, Kindle edition. Harper Collins E-Books, 2009. A good general overview of the subject.

Fehlau, Gunnar, Potter, Jeff (ed.). *The Recumbent Bicycle. Out Your Backdoor Press, 3rd edition*; 2006 (translated from the German and not updated). Focuses on the early history of recumbent bikes, and particularly on their record in racing.

Greene, Steve. *Free on Three: The Wild World of Human Powered Recumbent Tadpole Tricycles*. iUniverse 2011. A compilation of informative articles on different aspects of recumbent trikes by authorities and manufacturers in the field.

McCormack, Dale. *Safe Driving 4 Seniors: Enjoyment from Better Knowledge and Skills!* Institute for Traffic Safety 2017. Basically, a review of the basic rules of good driving, but adapted to the special needs of senior drivers.

Rye, Court. *A Practical Guide to Electric Bikes*, Kindle edition, Court Rye (publisher), 2014. An excellent introduction to the subject by the leading authority in this field.

Useful Digital Websites

Rollators

Just Walkers: https://www.wendyswalkers.com/. Lots of Information on walkers and rollators.

Mayo Clinic: https://www.mayoclinic.org/healthy-lifestyle/healthy-aging/multimedia/walker/sls-20076469. Excellent guide for the selection of a walker or rollator.

Wendy's Walkers: https://www.wendyswalkers.com/. Knowledgeable, honest, quick to fulfill orders. Site has much detailed information on walkers and rollators.

Recumbent Bikes and Trikes

Basically Bikes: https://basicallybicycles.com/. The site of a well-known and long-established recumbent bike dealer in Western Massachusetts. Full of information about trikes.

Bike-On: https://bike-on.com/.A Rhode Island-based firm that specializes in recumbent trikes, bikes and a large variety of other adaptive mobility machines. Knowledgeable, experienced and helpful staff.

BentRider Online: http://www.bentrideronline.com/. This is the pre-eminent domain for information about recumbent bikes.

Bicycleman: http://www.bicycleman.com/. The site of one of the oldest recumbent bike dealers. Full of information on all things concerned with trikes. You'll find reviews here can that you haven't found elsewhere. Highly recommended.

Hostel Shoppe: http://HostelShoppe.com/. Very helpful folks and very knowledgeable about all kinds of trikes. Much useful written information about trikes provided.

Laidback Bike Report: http://www.laidbackbikereport.com. Run by Gary Solomon, this is a monthly video report on the state of the trike world. The show, always stimulating, hosts many knowledgeable guests. Gary does a fine annual two-hour review of the Recumbent Cycle-Con Trade Show and Convention. https://www.recumbentcyclecon.com/.

Recumbent and Tandem Trike Magazine: http://www.rtrmag.com/. Full of excellent reviews, this is the trade magazine of the trike world.

Spike's Trikes: http://spikestrikes.biz/. Located in the Capital Region of New York, this is where I was first introduced to trikes. A premier Terratrike and Trident dealer who will spend hours seeing to it that you purchase a trike suitable for your particular needs.

Tadpole Rider: https://tadpolerider2.wordpress.com/. A really fine and detailed source of information on tadpole trikes in particular. Run by Steve Newbauer, it shows his dedication to the sport and hobby.

Trike Asylum: https://trikeasylum.wordpress.com/. Full of informative and entertaining videos about trikes, this too is a rich lode of information about them.

Utah Trikes: http://www.utahtrikes.com/. Another dealership with lots of information on site. In addition, it posts a series of informative videos on line.

Adult Trikes

Bicycle Riding for Boomers: http://www.bicycle-riding-for-boomers.com/step-through-bikes.html /. A good site with lots of information and specifications on adult bikes.

Adult Tricycle Reviews: http://adulttricyclereview.com/. A useful source of information on all sorts of tricycles. Definitely worth your time for some real in-depth reviews to be found here.

Electric Bikes

Bike Forums: https://www.bikeforums.net/electric-bikes/1128694-prodecotech-rebel-xs-vs-prodecotech-rebel-x-suspension.html/. The electric bike section of this forum is a good source of information as are the other sections devoted to various other kinds of bikes.

Electric Bike: https://www.electricbike.com/. Interesting site with some very good reviews and blogs.

Electric Bike Report: https://electricbikereport.com/ebike-news-more-ups-etrikes-costa-mesa-expo-husqvarna-pedelec-in-nyc-more-videos/. An e-bike trade journal, with good general information on the business side of e-bikes.

Electric Bike Review: https://www.electricbikereview,com/. The pre-eminent electric bike source. Its founder, Court Rye, does incredibly detailed written and video reviews of electric bikes. Its forums are full of knowledgeable and helpful folks—a crucial first stop for those interested in electric bikes.

Endless Sphere: https://endless-sphere.com/forums/. A site full of enthusiasts, but heavily slanted toward technical discussions of e-bikes.

Evelo Bikes: https://www.evelo.com/. Another commercial site that provides an excellent introduction to the electric bike world.

People for Bikes: http://peopleforbikes.org/. An advocacy and industry trade group for bikes, it closely follows e-bike developments and posts a map that chronicles the state-by-state status of e-bike laws.

Pedego Bikes: https://www.bikeforums.net/electric-bikes/1128694-prodecotech-rebel-xs-vs-prodecotech-rebel-x-suspension.html. This commercial site is full of general information about electric bikes.

State Electric Bicycle Laws: A Legislative Primer, National Conference of State Legislators December, 2016: http://www.ncsl.org/research/transportation/state-electric-bicycle-laws-a-legislative-primer.aspx/. Excellent source of info on state electric bicycle laws.

Senior Driving Resources

AAA: Senior Driving Resources: http://seniordriving.aaa.com/. This is an amazing site, full of essays and videos designed to help the senior driver stay on the road. For example, a self-rating test asks simple questions that, when tallied, tell you whether you are a safe or dangerous driver. Every question, whether answered correctly or not, comes with an essay that guides you to a preferred resolution of your driving problem. For example, in "Check Your Performance," one question might be: "I think I'm slower than I used to be in reacting to dangerous situations." Your answer might be, "Always, or almost always," "Sometimes," or "Never, or almost never."

The essay on this subject quietly suggests that your ability to react to danger depends on your hearing and sight remaining sharp. Then it subtly points out that both of these senses worsen with the onset of age. There follows a myriad of specific actions to help a driver worried about their failing skills: a senior driving course, taken either online or scheduled locally; further written tests; tests with a driver assessment specialist; daily exercise; and restricting driving to safe situations.

Included too on the site are pointers to brochures put out by the National Highway Traffic Safety Administration on subjects such as diabetes, arthritis, macular degeneration and sleep apnea and their effects on driving. Curative measures for these problems are suggested.

And there are instructions for very specific dangerous situations such as, "Making a left turn." Here the driver is urged to turn signals on at least 150 feet ahead of an intersection. Also, their specialists suggest going directly through an intersection that does not have a left turn signal and then making three right hand turns. This will permit you to come back to the intersection, but now with the light in your favor.

Much thought and work have gone into this site. Here you can also find segments devoted to physical fitness, car buying for seniors, and suggestions for alternatives to driving.

Particularly noteworthy is the link to Drive Sharp, https://www.drivesharp.com, a driving simulation and training program that claims it can "cut your risk of a car crash by up to 50 percent." Some AAA members receive a discount to this highly touted audio-visual program that takes them on a road trip and presents them with challenging situations.

And too there is a program called **Carfit**, https://www.car-fit.org/, jointly developed by AAA, AARP and AOTA (American Occupational Therapy Association) that through a free 20-minute inspection by a "Car Fit" technician will check out the senior driver's "fit" in the cockpit of the car. Proximity to the steering wheel and mirror adjustment are among the items covered in this brief but helpful service. A study of its pilot program back in 2005 concluded, for example, that almost 20 percent of the drivers "did not have a line of sight at least three inches over the steering wheel."

The Hartford and MIT AgeLab, "We Need to Talk":
http://www.thehartford.com/sites/thehartford/files/we-need-to-talk-2012.pdf/. This is a wonderful and highly detailed brochure that guides caregivers and concerned men and women in approaching a senior citizen who demonstrably needs to be removed from the road. From this same site, one can access several other well-written brochures: "Your Road Ahead: A Guide to Comprehensive Driving Evaluations;" "You and Your Car: A Guide to Driving Wellness;" "Your Road to Confidence: A Widow's Guide to Buying, Selling, and Maintaining a Car;" and "At the Crossroads: Family Conversations About Alzheimer's Disease, Dementia and Driving." Good and substantive reading for all senior drivers and for those who care about them!

AARP: https://www.aarp.org/auto/driver-safety/driving-assessment/. The AARP website, like the AAA site, is chock full of videos and short essays on the various problems of senior driving and solutions to them. Indeed, the above sites and the Hartford site often overlap in the sharing of resources for the senior driver. Here, among other helpful information, are again suggestions for approaching the senior driver when the dread day comes that they must be told to give up the keys, Indeed, there is an hour and a half interactive seminar on this subject.

It seems to me that a week or so spent by a senior driver on this site would be very helpful for it's full of interactive videos designed to ferret out one's shortcomings. After taking some of the tests, I, for one, am certain that I could have continued driving had it not been for my spinal stenosis. My reflexes are excellent; it's just that my body couldn't respond to them. Interestingly enough, a recent joint AAA and AOTA study shows that 90 percent of senior drivers don't take advantage of items, such as convex mirrors, seat cushions or pedal extensions that could make driving safer for them. Yet, drivers over 65 are twice as likely to be killed in an accident as younger drivers. See Long Road Study, AAA, November 29, 2017: http://newsroom.aaa.com/2017/11/90-percent-senior-drivers-dont-make-vehicle-adjustments-can-improve-safety/.

Recumbent Bike Manufacturers

Avenue Trikes: Avenue trikes.com/. A new manufacturer of an entry-level trike, distributed by the Bicycleman, a highly reputable dealership.

Azub Recumbents: https://azub.eu/. A high-level line of trikes manufactured in the Czech Republic.

Catrike Recumbents: https://www.catrike.com/. An American manufacturer renowned for the quality and workmanship of its trikes.

Greenspeed Recumbents: http://www.greenspeed.com.au/. An Australian firm, it's one of the oldest and most widely respected trike manufacturers.

Hase Trikes: https://hasebikes.com/12-1-news-homepage.html/. German manufacturer of sturdy and innovative Delta trikes.

HP Velotechnik: http://www.hpvelotechnik.com/index_e.html/. German manufacturer of a line of high quality trikes.

Ice Recumbent: http://www.icetrikes.co/. Pioneering British manufacturer of very popular and well-built trikes.

Pfiff: http://www.industrialbicycles.com/Piff.aspx/. German manufacturer of high quality semi-recumbent and "crank-forward" trikes.

Rans Bikes: http://www.ransbikes.com/. American manufacturer of high quality semi-recumbent "crank-forward" bikes.

Sun Bicycles: http://www.sun.bike/. A longtime American manufacturer of a variety of relatively affordable Delta and tadpole trikes.

Terratrike: http://www.terratrike.com/. An American manufacturer of entry-to-deluxe-level trikes that are both fairly inexpensive and user-accessible by virtue of the higher seat heights of many of its offerings.

Trident Trikes: tridenttrikes.com/. A worthy American competitor of Terratrike for the entry-level market. It has several very good folding offerings.

Van Raam: https://www.vanraam.com/en-gb/. Dutch manufacturer of well-built semi-recumbent bikes and trikes that are particularly suited for adaptive cycling.

Appendix

As a service to those who, like me, are returnees to cycling and are baffled by the multiplicity of gearing options, I've decided to tackle this problem head-on right here and now. After all, cycle gearing is not rocket science, and it's important, sooner or later, to understand its basics.

Let's begin with the dynamics of a single-speed bike. Up front, you pedal a chain around what's called a chainring. It has a number of teeth on it. This sends power to a toothed cog in the back that propels the back wheel or wheels, and the bike moves forward. Energy can neither be created nor destroyed!

But the bike will only go as fast as the power in your legs can move it. If you wanted to go any faster, you'd need a larger chainring with more teeth on it, thereby multiplying the power transmitted to the rear. But now, if you run into a hill, the going will be tough, and the bike will slow down. You'll need some way to get more revolutions out of each push of your leg.

In short, you'd have to downshift. If you can imagine that you have a car tachometer in front of you, you'd see the rpms shoot up. So, to conquer this hill, you would want a smaller chainring up front and a larger cog in back receiving the multiplied power. Thus, you'd now have many more revolutions in front, but be transmitting more intense climbing power to the back wheel. It would be going slow but steady. You'd be ascending that hill in style.

So, you know one thing now, that a smaller ring in the front when mated with the large ring in the back will always give you your maximum climbing power, but slower speed. Conversely, a larger ring in the front mated with a smaller ring in the back will always give you your fastest speed, but lowest climbing power. It's like an old-fashioned manual shift—you have to downshift to a lower gear to go up a hill but stay in high gear while you're cruising along the highway.

And logically enough, when you start to add chainrings up front—one or two is usual—and cogs (a set of multiple cogs is called a cassette) in the back, this relationship will hold through the entire pedaling routine. If you were to put the chain sequentially through all its gears, it would run in a straight line from (small in front, large in back equals slow and easy) all the way up to (large in front to small in back equals fast but hard).

Now, how does this translate to the numbers that you will normally see as you go shopping for your bike or trike? On a bike with a single chainring up front and a single cog in back, the number might read as 44-16t, 44 teeth up front and 16 teeth in the rear, giving you a good range to handle most ordinary terrain. Push the front up to 46, and you'd go faster and travel further per rotation, but it would feel harder than pedaling the 44-tooth chainring. Another way of figuring this out is that this is a 2.75 ratio. Increasing it to a 48t crank would move the ratio up to 3.0. You'd go faster, but work harder at it, and have initial slower acceleration. So that's how a single-speed bike operates.

Let's look at a typical configuration on a more complicated 27-speed Shimano derailleur system. It's called 27-speed because, in the front, there is a triple chainset with 50/39/30 chainrings and in the back nine cogs, ranging from 11 teeth to 34 teeth in size (11-34t).

What these numbers mean is that up front the largest ring, the fastest, will have 50 teeth, and the smallest one, the one you'll need to go up a hill, will have 30 teeth. Your in-between gear, which you'll use a lot, will have 39 teeth. Conversely, in the rear, your highest gear, the one you'll mate with the lowest (30) gear up front to go up hills has 34 teeth. Understanding this relationship is essential to conquering what's really a simple math problem.

What is the lowest hill-climbing gear you can use with this combination? Answer: the combination of the lowest ring, the 30 ring up front, with the 34-tooth cog in the back. Divide the front by the back and get a ratio of .88. Then simply multiply it by a 27-inch wheel size, an arbitrary historically derived figure always used in this calculation. Thus, .88 x 27=21. This final figure is called the gear inches—the distance that the 27-inch wheel would cover in one rotation. It gives you the lower end of your equation because remember, you're at the slowest part of our chainring-cassette combination.

Now, let's calculate how fast it can go, using the same formula, but different numbers. Up front, the biggest crank has 50 teeth, and in the back, the smallest of the nine cogs has 11 teeth. Divide 50/11 and you obtain a ratio of 4.54. You then take this number and multiply it by the arbitrary value of a 27-inch wheel and obtain a number of 123 gear inches for your highest speed. Thus, your total spread is 21-123, or 102 gear inches.

On a touring bike, a good ratio would be between 18 and 113 or 95 gear inches. Obviously, these numbers, arbitrarily taken from a cycling site would give you a better hill-climbing ability than would our example, but your top speed would be lower. At this point, your individual needs and intended purposes for cycling would come into play. So now, you have solved the problem of gear inches. The lower the number of gear inches, the better you can master a hill, the higher the number of gear inches, the faster you can go on the level and downhill. Incidentally, there are several good apps that will calculate the gear inches for you.

You're now over the hard part. What moves the chain in the front from left to right is a device called a front derailleur. It is controlled by levers called triggers or by a grip shift on the left handlebar. The same goes with the back derailleur, which is controlled by triggers or a grip shift on the right grip. Just remember, right for rear.

With what you've already learned, you should be able to catch on very quickly. As a matter of course, on basically level terrain, you should stay in the highest or middle gear up front and back, using the back gear to make modest changes, and the front gear when you want to make a major change, say from high to low as you come to rest at a stop sign.

For instance, you would be on the largest cog up front and the smallest in back and would move up the back cogs from 1 to 4 in general riding. Coming to a modest hill, you would shift down to the medium cog up front using the left-hand lever, then move to the middle cogs in the back, 4-5-6. In both instances, you would be in the middle. And, before you came to a complete stop, you'd shift down to the smallest front cog, and up to the largest cog or thereabouts in the rear, so you'd be in a low enough gear to start up again. You wouldn't want to be stuck in the biggest front crank and the smallest rear crank at this point in time because you'd find it hard to move off from the rest position.

At this point, I believe that we've covered all you need to know about this subject, but you'll likely learn more about it and other technical aspects of these marvelous machines as you come to enjoy the mobility they make possible.

Author's Note

Upon researching the subject of runners and the Central Park reservoir, it turns out that one Alberto Arroyo, a Puerto Rican-born New Yorker, began jogging around the reservoir sometime in the late 1930s. His obituary ran in the New York Times on March 26, 2010. The information on Aina Wifalk, the inventor of the rollator, was primarily gleaned from a February 29, 2016 article that appeared on the website of the Svenskt Uppfinnaire Museum, translated by Google.

Credits

The author thanks the manufacturers who supplied images of their vehicles for this book.

Fig. 10.1 Mission Cycles, Inc.
Fig. 10.2 Van Raam, Inc
Fig. 10.3 Photo by Allen B. Ballard
Fig. 10.4 PFIFF, Inc.
Fig. 10.5 Photo by Allen B. Ballard
Fig. 10.6 PFIFF, Inc.
Fig. 11.1 Cycling Without Age, Inc.

About the Author

**Allen Ballard**, a native of Philadelphia and a proud graduate of its Central High School, holds degrees from Kenyon College and Harvard University. He's a retired professor from CCNY and the University of Albany. The prize-winning author of three other non-fiction books and two novels, he, at age 87, still maintains a daily exercise routine of walking, upper-body workouts, and indoor and outdoor cycling. He lives in Clifton Park, New York, and is a great fan of the Adirondacks and, in particular, its crown jewel, Lake George, where he first went to work as a busboy at its Silver Bay YMCA resort at the age of 16. He still visits it yearly, but not to work!

CPSIA information can be obtained
at www.ICGtesting.com
Printed in the USA
LVHW071503160419
614375LV00019B/1121/P

9 781945 146497